James Occhipinti is one of t[illegible] people [illegible] pastor looks for. He's very smart, a naturally gifted leader, and an obedient servant of the Lord. I am constantly impressed with his willingness to serve and his desire to help others find the same fulfillment in lay ministry. As one of the key lay leaders at Saddleback Church James was a standout, always ready and willing to serve, talented in a myriad of ways, and a highly effective leader and teacher. He exemplifies the heart of our faith by not just professing the value of servanthood, but leading by example.

The mark of a good leader is how many people are following them. The church moves not on the feet of the pastors, but on the strength of its lay leadership. James Occhipinti's wisdom and his walk with Christ have brought many strong new leaders into lay ministry. I am delighted that he has codified all of this into an enlightening and inspiring book that encourages and strengthens every believer to be the hands and feet of Christ. May his example and his teaching mobilize you into a lifetime you never imagined, one that God has predestined for you. Our world desperately needs you. By reading and applying James' words, you can help change the world for the better, and be forever changed in the process.

- **Ron Wilbur**,
Pastor, Saddleback Church (retired)

The Call to ministry is A to Z. It is not simply A and B, pastors and missionaries only. While the Call to vocational ministry is cardiac for the church and culture, the Call to ministry for every person is critical if we expect to carry out the Great Commission of Jesus in our lifetime. In fact, one could make the obvious claim that lay persons will influence more people for the kingdom of God than clergy will ever think about reaching. Our young adults need to know that God wants to utilize their livesnow. It's the same for older adults, too. James Occhipinti not only writes about the importance of lay persons knowing about their ministry and leadership influence for Christ, he lives it out on a daily basis. This content is long overdue in a world that will need every follower of Jesus to be his hands and feet wherever he places us.

**- Dr. Jim Dunn**,
President Oklahoma Wesleyan University

The calling to lay ministry is as real and important as any calling in the kingdom of God. I have seen James endeavor to work his lay ministry calling out in a real and meaningful way, writing this book is a great testament to his dedication to fulfilling his calling and willingness to do something bold for the church. From working to further the the mission of Christian Higher Education, serving to lead and foster healthy Community Group ministries and serving as a Missionary Pilot in Mexico, James has lived out his calling and continues to seek out the narrow path.

**- Dr. Jim Garlow**,
CEO, Well Versed

"James Occhipinti knows that no team wins if the majority of the players sit on the sidelines. 'Who's Job Is It?' is a clarion call to get off the bench and get in the game. Victory is everyone's job! No one can sit this one out."

**- Dr. Everett Piper,**
President Emeritus, Oklahoma Wesleyan University.
Columnist and Best Selling Author

Only a few of us are called to full-time ministry as Pastors, but all of us are called to utilize our God-given gifts for kingdom advancement. As believers, out of gratitude and faith we arecompelled to service and to share the good news of God's redeeming love. "Every Member a Minister" offers inspiringexamples, encouragement, and exhortation that is grounded in scripture and illustrated with practical stories that will inspire your life calling to practical everyday service. This book will stir your passion to get involved with God's ongoing life transforming team of ministers in a compelling, winsome way. As James points out – Dare to Imagine – then live out God's calling for your life – you won't regret it!

**- Dr. Yorton Clark,**
Business Professor/Academic Dean MidAmerica Nazarene University

# Whose Job is it Anyway?

## A VIEW FROM THE PEW

JAMES OCCHIPINTI

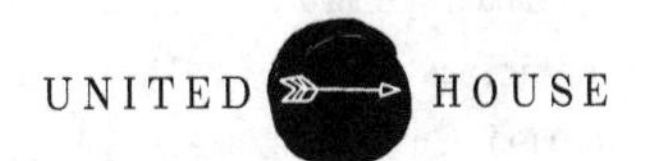

Published by UNITED HOUSE Publishing



ISBN: 978-1-952840-46-3

UNITED HOUSE Publishing - Waterford, Michigan
info@unitedhousepublishing.com | unitedhousepublishing.com

Interior design: Matt Russell, Marketing Image, mrussell@marketing-image.com

Printed in the United States of America (2024—First Edition)

*I would be remis if I didn't dedicate this book to Pastor Rick Warren, my Pastor for almost 20 years. I must admit I went to Saddleback Church kicking and screaming! My wife Valerie drug me by the ear and I reluctantly succumb to her insistence. It's not as if I had any reservations about the theology being taught, that is as biblically sound as it could possibly be and I certainly had no issues with Pastor Rick or the many other Pastors and administrators. My issues were simple, I am and always will be a small church guy, simply put, the mega church intimidated me and I resisted. Our Saddleback small group of over 17 years became the small church I needed.*

*In the end, Pastor Rick won me over and I never looked back. Pastor Rick's teaching every week was simply mesmerizing, I found myself taking notes like a kid in seminary and in the end it was those sermon notes filed with Rick-isms and wisdom that fill's these pages, the spiritual wisdom I gained from sitting in that audience every week and serving in ministry under Pastor Rick's direction is and always will be a blessing to me and my family.*

# Table of Contents

# Introduction: "Every Member a Minister"

Please note: Some may say this book is not for everyone, but I disagree. The less spiritually energetic may feel that if you are not a Christian attending church regularly, involved in a ministry, and growing in your faith, or at least desiring to do so, you may not grasp the concept of this book. I implore you to rethink that and consider embracing a more fulfilling and committed approach to your faith. This book may provide a bridge to get you there. In writing these pages, it is my sincere desire to motivate and bless you with Biblical truths rather than confuse or even offend you, depending on where you are in your spiritual journey. This book is for all believers, and I propose it might be life-changing for you.

I have had the honor and blessing of attending and serving at Saddleback Church for the last two decades. My reflection on Saddleback's ministry and the blessing it has been in my life, the lives of my family, and the lives of many of my dearest friends is nothing less than astonishing.

Consider the opening sentence of *The Purpose Driven Life*, written by the founding Pastor at Saddleback Church, Rick Warren: "It's NOT all about you."[1] Now, words mean something, and I suggest we change the emphasis toward our calling by God because it really is all about YOU; it really is all about everyone who calls themselves a follower of Christ, and here's why. Throughout Biblical history and in our world today, God uses His people to do His work. God used Jesus

(God incarnate) to deliver His message of love, forgiveness, and salvation, and to ultimately pay the final wage for sin. God used Moses to deliver His people from bondage after 430 years under Pharaoh and to part the Red Sea. He used John the Baptist to prepare the Jewish people for the coming of Jesus Christ. He used the disciples to deliver the saving message of Jesus as Christ to the world. God routinely ordains men and women from every ethnicity, creed, color, and economic circumstance to carry out His work. Perhaps the best example, in modern times, is how He has used Pastor Rick every day, in my opinion, as this generation's most influential pastor and writer.

God has used many throughout the ages to carry His message and do His work; Paul, Mother Teresa, and Florence Nightingale are just a few. Often, these people are not the usual suspects; they aren't seminary graduates, great theologians, or Old or New Testament scholars. God used fishermen, tax collectors, pastors, popes, salesmen, and slave traders, throughout the ages, to do His work. Noah was a drunk, Abraham was too old, Isaac was a daydreamer, Jacob was a liar, Leah was unlovely, Joseph was abused, Moses was very meek and had a stuttering problem, Gideon was afraid, Samson had long hair and was a womanizer, Rahab was a prostitute, Jeremiah and Timothy were too young and filled with doubt, David was an adulterer and a murderer, Elijah was suicidal, Isaiah preached naked, Jonah ran from God, Naomi was a widow, Job went bankrupt, John the Baptist ate bugs and was unwashed, Peter denied Christ, the disciples fell asleep while praying, Martha worried about everything, and the Samaritan woman was divorced (more than once). Are you seeing the pattern? I would imagine your perceived flaws or excuses pale in contrast to most of God's biblical heroes. It takes courage to embrace your calling. Are you willing to be used? Are you courageous enough to claim your calling from God?

There is a calling God has for you and for all who are

ready to serve. The process of divine calling has changed in our generation. Callings are not just for pastors and priests or vocational ministers and missionaries but for every follower. Romans 8:29-30, repeats several times that we are all ordained and predestined. The Calvinist and Arminian theologians can debate the pure definition of predestination, but let's all agree that God calls us. At some point in history, Biblical direction gave way to vocational ministry dominating service. In the book of Acts, the church is illustrated as a small group of believers preaching, teaching, and worshiping in homes and other gathering places. As the typical church has evolved over the last 25-30 years into a much different-looking ministry, we, as believers, need to embrace our calling to meet new challenges. It is important for us to be open to the Holy Spirit's direction as the needs of the church change.

We, as Christians, have become very comfortable in our church pews, our seats in the rented school auditorium, or wherever we worship. Christians have acquired the check-writing view of offering plate stewardship—we simply drop a $20 bill in the offering plate and now God's work is someone else's problem; after all, what am I paying for? Where does the money go, and what is the money used for? Well, those may be very good questions, perhaps left to be answered at another time. Our focus needs to be taking back our jobs as Christian soldiers, fulfilling our "purpose," and accepting our calling to act on it. In the following chapters, we will explore our responsibility as Christians, lay ministers, and lay leaders with a purpose: God's purpose!

Now, before I go any further, I want to make it clear and without question that I love and respect Rick Warren. I believe God has given this generation the gift of Rick Warren, in the same way He gave my parents' generation the gift of the late Billy Graham. Throughout the ages, God has gifted His people with wise and dedicated people to carry His message and do His work, and that is precisely my point. Oh, and by the way, I do agree with Pastor Rick's statement, "It's not about us," in the context of *The Purpose Driven Life*. With the blessing of more than fifty-five million copies sold, I assume God agrees too. Much of the inspiration for writing this book comes from sitting with the Saddleback Church congregation each week and absorbing the ordained words of this great pastor along with all the others called to serve at Saddleback Church. Most of my context is based on the sermon notes I feverishly take each week.

Before we move into the chapters, please reflect on what defines you. The answer for me has evolved over the years. My title at work was a very big deal to me in my early career, and it was something I used to define who I was. I am in my fifties now, and I have had a few titles in my day. I have been called a student, graduate, husband, father, Second Lieutenant, First Lieutenant, Captain, Commander, First Officer, teacher, supervisor, manager, director, principal, vice president, president, trustee, elder, non-executive director, Chief Pilot, Chief Operating Officer, Chief Executive Officer, and now author. What I now know is that none of these titles define me. They don't help you get to know me, and most of all, none of these titles are who I am. They simply tell you what I did or currently do to make a living.

As Christians, who we are can only be defined by who calls us. We can only be defined by our purpose and who gave it to us. To truly know me is to know my purpose and my calling. To truly know me is to know I am driven, I am a risk-taker, and I am an extrovert. I am passionate and a bit obsessed with a few things: my family, my friends, my business, cars, airplanes, and my calling—God's purpose for my life. To really, really know me is to know that God's call on my life cements the rest of those things together and defines me. Do you know what defines, what cements you?

ONE

# Calling - Your Value, His Vision

Values or value: Though similar, the words have two very different meanings. I would argue that unless you value your values, you won't step out and work for what you believe in. In other words, is your salvation so important to you that you must share it with others? Is your life so drastically different that you want everyone you know to have the same experience? Are you brave enough to accept your calling? I don't mean stand on a corner, beat a drum, and preach to the passersby. Will you share your whole life with those around you and strive to serve God, no matter your circumstances? These are the questions we must ask ourselves as we cast our vision and determine what defines us. We must ask a few simple questions: Do we understand our value? Are we living a life of value? Do we desire others to see us as valuable? Are we facilitating value in others? In my experience, this is where God will really work in us. If our job is the most important thing to us, then He will expect us to put it on the line. If our home is where we place our value, then He expects us to deed it to Him and use it to His glory. God knows our hearts. He knows our struggles, and it is precisely there where He will redirect our focus to His mission.

My journey in truly distinguishing the differences and relevance between the optional definitions for value began over thirty years ago while attending chapel services at Oklahoma Wesleyan University. Like most students at faith-based Christian universities, we were required to attend weekly chapel service, where the school's chaplain would either lecture on the Biblical topic of the week or invite a guest speaker to do the same. Where I found myself, most of the time, was hiding under a hoodie with the university's logo, trying to sleep during the inconveniently early time slot between early morning and mid-morning classes. Christian mission, and its application to my life, were foreign territory for me, at that time. I wound up at a Christian university for no other reason than to play ball. My high school grades, though not atrocious, were average at best, and they were certainly not good enough to elevate me above others when competing for athletic scholarships. I was an above-average athlete with below-average grades who needed a break to get into a good college. Fortunately, my coach since junior high, who was one of the biggest influences in my life, had a brother who was a professor and a coach at Oklahoma Wesleyan University. I was handed my break, my miracle, in the form of an acceptance letter and scholarship. Through the influence and witness of Coach Whitehouse, I accepted Jesus Christ as my Lord and Savior when I was a freshman in high school. When we invited Coach Whitehouse to our home for dinner recently, we discussed all of the details surrounding my acceptance to Oklahoma Wesleyan, and I'm not sure he even knows how he pulled it off. I'm sticking with the miracle explanation.

## Calling - Your Value, His Vision

Upon my arrival at college, I was an eighteen-year-old California beach kid wearing Sperry Top-Sider shoes and Levi's 501 button-up jeans, sitting smack dab in the middle of the Bible belt, with no real understanding of what I was in for spiritually. Week after week, we heard preachers and missionaries talking about their spiritual journeys. Spiritual journey? I didn't even know there was such a thing. My spiritual journey consisted of mandatory mass attendance with my father and praying, "Now I lay me down to sleep . . . " at bedtime as a child. I went to church, and my parents said we were Christians, so for me, my Christianity was more about claiming club membership than anything else.

Baby steps are important at this point in my faith journey. Back in Oklahoma, week after week, I began to realize these people in front of the chapel were talking about faith much richer and deeper than I'd experienced. There was a foundational commitment much stronger than I claimed, and most importantly, there was a grounded sense of calling on their lives that seemed unquenchable. The more I heard, the more it scared me, and the more scared I was, the more I responded with denial. Little did I know, this was my first introduction to the Holy Spirit in a real and meaningful way, and frankly, it would take me quite some time to fully understand the impact those chapel services had on me and my spiritual journey. To this day, I credit those biweekly mandatory impositions as formative to my true understanding of the calling on my life and really valuing my values.

Looking back, understanding there was a calling on my life was as basic as 1, 2, 3. I now realize belief in God and His calling on us is imprinted in all of us. It's in our DNA, much like the instinct to breathe or the feeling of hunger or thirst. The truth of God is written on our hearts, and our calling is given to us as sustenance for a life lived as intended by God.

Oswald Guinness, Ph.D., perhaps one of the foremost intellectuals in Christian thought today, puts it like this in his book *The Call*: There are three basic families of faiths, or "sources of everything," competing for our basic need of purpose and calling: Eastern religions (Buddhism, Hinduism, and Sikhism amongst others), Secular Humanism (Atheism, Utilitarianism, Ethical Naturalism, and Evolutionists), and Biblical Judeo Christianity.[2] Islam fits in the latter because of its roots with Abraham, though clearly, Islam has so splintered from Judeo-Christianity that it is now unrecognizably kin.

Guinness, in essence, reveals that though there are many forms of Eastern thought; you can boil them all down to a single principle: "We are meaningless, our purpose is meaningless, and our calling is meaningless." Only after we fully understand our identity is as meaningless as the ant walking on a sidewalk, will we reach nirvana, after many incarnations of life (up to 18,000). As I see the world through the Eastern-religious lens, the disregard for human worth and personal meaning is clear. I have traveled the world; I've been to the Taj Mahal in India, where the crowd of beggars is so thick you can hardly navigate the property. I've seen the Tōdai-ji in Nara, Japan, where culturally, people are simply reduced to the amount of work they can accomplish. I have driven on the streets of Mumbai, India, where the homeless situation is so bad, people need to sleep vertically on the sidewalk because there is not enough room for everyone to sleep horizontally.

I have seen the East's abject disregard for human life. In Eastern cultures, children are enslaved for sex, families sell their young girls because of their street value, and to get as much productivity as possible, grown men are made to sleep on the streets next to their construction jobs to earn just pennies a day. I see the Eastern cultures with wealth, great natural resources, and very good education systems, which are free to everybody, but their society lacks a basic value for human life. Citizens are forced to drink, bathe, and defecate in local rivers because of the lack of infrastructure—lack of running water and sanitation—capabilities that have been around since the Roman Empire.

I have spent a lot of time in countries like India, Sri Lanka, and China; these societies do not lack the resources or ability to provide the most basic needs to their citizens. Instead, they lack the willingness to see value in their citizens as people of God and individuals, thus failing to provide the most basic standards of living. If your culture sees you as meaningless, and if you see yourself as meaningless, you inevitably see everybody else around you as meaningless. It is this kind of thinking that motivates the thoughts of Guinness.

Guinness says Secular Humanism is equally foreboding but takes you to the opposite extreme. Humanists say there is no God, no judgment, no good or bad. There are simply time, space, cells, proteins, DNA, and RNA that form and evolve, so it is up to us to make the best of them and blaze our own trail. We are to "take the bull by the horns," and use what is in front of us. It's all a matter of chance.[3] Richard Dawkins, the modern theorists' demigod of Oxford University, boils it down so eloquently in his book *The God Delusion*, "It is all dumb luck."[4] Bertrand Russell, one of the most famous humanists of the last century and perhaps the father of modern Secular Humanism, could be summarized thus: We must take the world on our shoulders, like the Greek god Atlas, and carry it ourselves. We will own our purpose, and in the end, our calling is to ourselves.

Secular Humanism was the most alluring to me. But, there is more than one glitch with it. It is almost impossible for me to stand back in any type of academic reasoning and think like an "intellectual." Here is what I mean: Can I really believe that everything around me is because of a couple of cells colliding and portions folding and mating between 4.5 and 8.5 billion years ago?; that the perfect union and symbiotic universe was and is an accident, a mere collision in a black hole, somewhere back in time, with the force to create everything? For me, a reality check was in order, and the one in one to the between 26th and 123rd power chance (IBM Supercomputer) that life is an accident takes way too much faith from me.

I find it interesting that the scientific community embraces the Big Bang Theory when explaining the creation of the Earth as absolute fact, even though it defies the most basic scientific principles that define scientific proof. In science, the proof of a principle of science requires repeatable and predictable empirical data and evidence, or, in other words, only when you can repeat an experiment and keep getting the same result is that principle considered scientifically sound. To my knowledge, this "Big Bang" has never been repeated, never been substantiated, and its evidence is only a grand presumption in theory. Equally, the scientific community, as a whole, has embraced Darwin's self-admitted errors as scientific facts. Darwin stretched his theory from adaptation (God-given ability for His creation to adapt and prosper) of a species to evolution from one kind of a species to another.

In other words, the adaptation of a species illustrated is the change over time from a Bobcat in Texas having a short coat to a Bobcat in Canada having long fur. Based on survival within an ecosystem, adaptation is both repeatable and predictable, and it meets all of the criteria to be scientific fact. Where the problem occurs for the secular humanist is evolution—the change from one kind of species to another, such as an ape to a human being. There is NO scientific or observable evidence that any kind of species has turned into a different kind of species. Secular Humanists must embrace the faith of evolution because the change from one species to another has no evidence, just theory or "faith." Thus, this led to the court decision *McCreary County v. ACLU, 545 U.S. 844*, in 2005, which decided that Secular Humanism met the standard definition of a religion, as defined in the Establishment Clause of the Constitution of the United States of America.[5]

In the end, it would take me a little time with the Holy Spirit to really embrace my true calling and Biblical Christianity on a spiritual level. For me, stepping out in faith, in the beginning, was more about what club I wanted to be a part of and which philosophies I believed to be the most genuine. I saw the world like this: the Eastern religions offered me a hamster wheel of trial and failure, spinning round and round from life to life, only to never really satisfy my deep desire to realize my purpose. I saw Secular Humanism as a similar spinning wheel, getting me nowhere, except for obtaining a few positions, degrees, or titles, but accomplishing very little for the greater good. It appeared to me that any real or lasting contributions Secular Humanism made to the world, at large, were from institutions that they squatted on, confiscated, and re-missioned away from Judeo-Christianity.

Here is what I mean: Though Secular Humanism takes claim to and credit for education, and more notably higher education, it was the church that brought education to the people of the world in an ubiquitous way. Even notable institutions have founding mottos, such as Harvard: "Veritas Christo et Ecclesiae—Truth for Christ and the Church," Yale: "Lux et Veritas—Light and Truth," and Princeton: "Dei Sub Numine Viget—Under the Protection of God She Flourishes." These were all started by the church. In fact, all of the Ivy League schools began as church schools of higher learning and were, predominantly, for spiritual seminary teaching. Brown University, with the founding motto "In Deo Speramus—In God we Hope," ironically enough, was chartered under Baptist roots and was the first to admit students from any Christian religion, not just Puritan high churches. Brown's founder, Roger Williams, "a Calvinist in Outlook," believed that no civil authority had the right to interfere with religious belief, so he created Brown as an open alternative to the "prestigious Puritan Church Schools." Oh, how the Secular Humanists have aborted the founding principles of these once righteous-minded institutions.

How many legacy hospitals in your community

begin with the word Saint or end with the word Methodist or Presbyterian? Secular Humanism has obfuscated science and medicine to the degree that any dissenters in these fields are rebuked, even in these ministry institutions. The list goes on and on. Orphanages, food banks, homeless shelters, and charities of all types were created because of long-forgotten Christians acting on their callings. These people, who dedicated their lives to serving others in the name of Jesus, have been confiscated by Secular Humanism and, in turn, lost their first love.

In contrast, I had to ask myself, what has Secular Humanism done for the greater good on its own? I looked around and found virtually nothing done in the name of atheism or Secular Humanism (created for service to mankind). Sure, in some way, we can point to the green movements attempting to "save the planet from man," but it's a drop in the bucket and filled with contradiction compared to the influence the Holy Spirit has had on the world. Also, in this realization, it became very apparent to me that Secular Humanism, Biblical Judeo-Christianity, and Eastern religions all serve a god. Every human has it imprinted on their soul to serve God. I needed to ask myself, "What god was I to serve?" I needed to figure out who I would allow to take claim of my soul. Accepting and living for the Almighty and living God through the Trinity was a no-brainer. A calling to serve the Creator of the universe was icing on the cake.

Sidebar: I'm a bit of a physics nerd and am interested in everything aerospace, so as with most people interested in flight and space, I find myself drawn to the science channel and its episodes about the solar system and the creation of Earth. The blind acceptance of theory is most interesting to me. It resembles our school board passing off ketchup as a vegetable while it's missing some key components, like really being a vegetable. Like most deceptions, they are wrapped in a compelling amount of fact and a touch of truth. Like ketchup, almost everything we have been taught about the history of deep space and the beginning of the universe is theory or the ideas of theoretical physicists.

Don't get me wrong; I am not saying the physicists are completely wrong, nor are all of their theories wrong—no, obviously not. But, back to the ketchup comparison: When we mix a little fact and a little reality with a lot of creativity, we get a perverted view of what is true. The truth is, almost everything we know and have been led to believe about space and time, black holes, the beginning of the universe, the Big Bang, and evolution is Secular Humanist theory with very little scientific fact or quantifiable proof. I find it amazing how our theoretical physicists espouse their theories as fact, and the scientific community eats it up with the same fervor as a Scientologist eats up the fictional sci-fi writings of L. Ron Hubbard, the late author of Scientology.

The truth is, for Secular Humanism to exist, it must feed on theory and supposition—on faith. The research arm of the higher education industry is a great example. Without great theories based on some fact and much supposition, there is no grant money. With no grant money, there is no money to build buildings or to pay salaries, and no money for really cool toys to further explore these theories. And probably, most importantly, in the higher education industry, there is no money to fuel the intellectual peer review process where the "intellectuals" prop each other up and celebrate each other's theories. In the end, the Secular Humanist illusion must continue so their institutions stay relevant, financially solvent, and their employees stay employed, remembering all along that most of what is being preached by the Secular Humanist is theory and not even close to proven.

More and more, we are hearing from the defectors of intellectual elitism. Interestingly enough, the scientific community is amongst the largest professional communities defecting to Christianity. Many of these people are waking up to the fraud that Secular Humanism is perpetrating.

For me, if I have a calling, then it must matter, and the genesis of that calling must be worthy and true. God is worthy and true—all else is simply a perversion of reality.

## TWO

# Calling Requires Leadership

Even if you don't see yourself as a leader, God does. *Authority* and *leadership* are words that make many of us tremble. As committed Christians, we are called to authority and leadership in one form or another. It is a role we are created to play. At Saddleback, Pastor Rick reveals, week after week, that there is a vacuum we must fill, a predestined responsibility if you will. Our calling was created by God from the beginning of time, and, well before we were born, God equipped us with a purpose. He prepared everything we needed to carry out His perfect plan. Are we imperfect? Yes! Do we step outside of that perfect plan from time to time? Yes! And that is okay, for God sees us as sinless and without blame through the gift of grace through Jesus. In realizing my imperfections, I'm reminded of the old adage, those who live in glass houses should not throw stones. Aren't we all made of glass, and don't we all live in a glass house? Even though we are stained and a little chipped or broken, we are all called to service with authority and leadership.

*You are worthy, our Lord and God, to receive glory and honor and power, for you created all things, and by your will they were created and have their being.*
Revelation 4:11, NIV

We are created to serve. Nobody comes as an empty

shell or as a bystander. We all have a purpose, which is why we are all important in the plans of God. There is one thing I know for sure: I would never reach out and serve on my own. I am just not built that way—I'm not that thoughtful, not that caring, and I'm not confident that I could or would make a difference. Whether you were born to serve and find it completely natural, or like me, it is a learned trait, service to God must be selfless and not pompous. It must be carried out with the understanding that service is for His glory and not ours, and we must always remember He created us for His purpose, and He will equip us in His providence.

God has never committed any assignment to man without backing him with His authority, which is why He is not necessarily looking for the wise or the ready-made. God uses those who make themselves available for His use. With God, sometimes it's as easy as raising your hand and saying, "Present." Wherever you are when God calls you, He can make and mold you into what He wants you to be.

*But you will receive power when the Holy Spirit comes on you; and you will be my witnesses in Jerusalem, and in all Judea and Samaria, and to the ends of the earth.*
Acts 1:8, NIV

Wielding the authority we have in Christ is very important because that is the only way we can overcome the enemies around us. He knows what we are up against, the type of havoc they can wreak, and the right weapons and strategy that can effectively counter them.

*And these signs will accompany those who believe: In my name they will drive out demons; they will speak in new tongues; they will pick up snakes with their hands; and when they drink deadly poison, it will not hurt them at all; they will*

*place their hands on sick people, and they will get well.*
Mark 16:17-18, KJV

## Develop Your WHY and Use it Without Fear

Christianity is not just a religion or a movement, it is a new life altogether—a new life in Christ, which is the highest form of life man can discover and live. Think about this for a moment: We enjoy an active life with Christ now, as we prepare for an eternity in Heaven. God could have just left well enough alone and said, "The world is lost, and my creation is on its own until I call them to Heaven." But no; God decided He wants fellowship with us now. He wants us to prepare for heaven now so we can see a glimpse of eternity in this life. Life with God now is so important that Jesus Christ Himself came to earth to lead us and prepare us—to take on the sin of the world.

God desires fellowship with us now. Not later, *now*! I must admit, I was a Christian for a very long time before I truly understood the power and sheer gravity of Jesus' death on the cross. I used to think people gave up their lives for others all the time. Firemen rush into burning buildings, soldiers routinely perform selfless acts so citizens can enjoy the God-given freedoms we take for granted, and as a parent, I can almost assuredly say I would take a bullet for one of my girls, as most of you would. But to see Christ's death as merely dying for our sins is missing the real sacrifice. The real story is found in the Garden of Gethsemane, where Jesus prepared for his pending doom. It wasn't death Jesus toiled over. It was the weight of taking on the "sin of the world." Can you imagine the emotion, the pain, and the confusion the acceptance of that responsibility would bring? There are no words to describe it.

THREE

# God's Influence - Use It!

Our personal influence is critical to God's plan; our service is multiplied by our influence. Christian service is a life man cannot learn or achieve on his own. It is given by God through the Holy Spirit. Everyone who has accepted Christ will have access to this life and will be able to receive all the blessings that come with it. I have seen it and lived it. The key to finding true happiness is to serve.

*The thief comes only to steal and kill and destroy;*
*I have come that they may have life, and have it to the full.*
John 10:10, KJV

God uses us to spread more than just His Word—He uses us to show His love and to live His love with those around us. We have to share the life of Christ with others, including the rejected and the condemned. Not just the condemned and the broken, but the rich and famous as well. Those who seem on top of the world have the same spiritual needs as the poor man, and as we know through 24/7 tabloid access, the rich and famous are perhaps the most dispirited when it comes to religious relationships. This is because they, out of all of us, may realize that wealth, and/or fame, do not translate into happiness.

Now, God does use the rich as well as the poor to complete His will. One evening during our small group study, we were talking about wealth as a Christian. Can a rich man really serve God and make it into heaven? The question was appropriately asked by one of my best friends, a man who has truly been blessed financially and is now without the pressures of work or bills. During the discussion and an examination of Scripture, it became clear God uses all to fulfill His purpose. Think about it: Who would witness to the Bill Gates' of the world if it weren't for wealthy believers who are willing to be used by God? Like it or not, cultural dynamics place us in circles that are usually defined by our economic status. I'm pretty sure Bill Gates isn't hanging out with many poor pastors or missionaries at his country club. God uses His people in every station of life to reach those around them. Thankfully, God's love is not just reserved for the poor; it is available to all who accept it.

In God's eyes, none are beyond redemption. Even while hanging on the cross, Jesus saved one of the condemned criminals nailed to the cross next to Him. Man rejected the criminal, but God accepted him when he repented of his sins. Contrary to many other religions, Christian witness is not achieved by force or tyranny. God usually brings people to know Him through relationships with other believers, including pastors and missionaries. There is a renaissance within Christianity today—a realization of personal ministry—using our personal influence to reach those around us with the love of Christ. Our influence through relationships is critical to God's work and to our purpose. Our influence and relationships connect our friends with the new life we have received, as they see us living out our faith. Your willingness to live out your faith is sometimes all it takes to reveal the Lordship of Christ in their lives. Through miracles and His witness, Jesus used his power of influence to show the will of God, and He calls us to do the same.

## God's Influence - Use it!

*In the same way, let your light shine before others, that they may see your good deeds and glorify your Father in heaven.*
Matthew 5:16, ESV

God works in many wondrous ways, but what can not be disputed—second only to the miracle of Jesus Christ—is the power of God's hand through the hand of Christians everywhere who say, "Yes, Lord. Use me." It is said we are the "light of the world," and our good works show the people of the world the great love of Jesus Christ. God has put the power in the life of every believer to shine across the world. God uses Christians to show hope in the darkness of everyday humanity.

FOUR

# Calling Requires Influence

Jesus is a model for influencing people. When Jesus was present on earth, people reacted. As Jesus returned to Jerusalem, the crowds reacted, the Pharisees reacted, and the disciples reacted. He did not always receive a welcome reception, but He did influence everybody around Him. The crowds first saw Jesus as a miracle worker and someone who could meet their needs; a "what's in it for me?" mindset prevailed, which led to their cries to crucify Him.

*. . . Hosanna! Blessed is he who comes in the name of the Lord. Blessed is the King of Israel.*
John 12:13, NIV

*When the crowds realized that Jesus was not going to do what they wanted they turned on him . . . they shouted, "Take him away! Take him away! Crucify him!"*
John 19:15, NIV

The religious leaders of the day were very comfortable and wanted to maintain the status quo. They had control, and they possessed wealth—a bad combination to go up against for someone sent to change the world. All in all, Jesus' influence was received as both good and bad by those in His presence. There is a huge lesson to be learned from the authority Jesus demonstrated. It was consistent: He never wavered from God's will or direction. Jesus used His influence for good and for God, not to win favor and not to make friends or make everybody happy. If we use our voice for God, we run the risk of offending some and of standing in the face of political correctness. That's okay. Serving is sometimes uncomfortable.

### Jesus is Foundationally Prayerful

As we set out to influence through God and for God, it is important to keep Him as an integral part of the process. I strive to make prayer perpetual and not just something I do when I happen to remember or only at a set time every day. We need to be praying as we take the curves in our day.

I am reminded of a chance encounter I once had with a homeless man and the significance of prayer, or the lack of it, in the process. In this particular case, I fell short. After service at Saddleback one Sunday morning, I was met with an empty tank of gas as we made our way from church. In an attempt to minimize our tardiness, I pushed the envelope and stretched the tank to fumes by going to service before the gas station. It is a cardinal sin for a pilot to run out of gas, and I knew the potential for humiliation and ridicule, but this time, the gamble paid off.

While filling my tank, I was interrupted by a man who approached me from behind and asked for a few extra dollars so he could put gas in the car that he was living in with his wife and his son. Confession—I am instantly skeptical of young, able-bodied individuals who ask for money because, in my experience, they tend to be financing their next fix or bottle. I realized the young man seemed different though—he had clearly slept in the clothes he was wearing, and there was no outward sign of a scam. I gave him all the cash I had in my wallet.

I looked over at his wife and son sitting in the car with

the windows rolled up and saw they were looking down and not interactive; it appeared to me they were either too ashamed to look at me or they were praying as they sought help from others. As I finished pumping my gas, I decided to use my credit card to fill his car up and chat with him a little. I told him I would like to give him a blessing. Our conversation was strained—I could tell he was very embarrassed and not very chatty. He was giving me one-word answers, but I did get out of him that they were living in the Walmart parking lot and they were safe and fed. He quickly thanked me and told me I was a blessing. I could see the gratefulness in his eyes as the gas pump clicked off, and he hurriedly went on his way.

I had at least two opportunities to pause and pray, but I didn't. I should have after I gave him the cash, and I should have before I walked over to fill his gas tank. It was only after I drove off that I prayed for him and his family, and only after driving several miles, knowing the man and his family would have now moved on, that I heard from God what I should have done.

Now, at first glance, perhaps I should feel pretty good about myself. I relieved him of the stress of finding fuel for at least a week and, hopefully, gave him the ability to be mobile and find a job. Only after praying, though, did I realize the additional opportunities I'd had to provide assistance. Less than a mile away was the Saddleback Church food bank, where he could have stocked up on food. Also less than a mile away was the Saddleback Church Peace Center, where the family could have tapped into the many resources offered to people in such need, including temporary housing, financial assistance, and spiritual counseling. This was all less than a mile away, and in my strength, I blew it.

The truth is, I was so preoccupied with how to tell the man about Jesus that I missed an opportunity to show him Jesus. A simple prayer *before* I acted could have made a big difference for him and his family. It's kind of funny how need is all around us, but as we do what we do, we tend to miss so much. My wife Valerie was five feet away from this whole encounter, and she didn't even know it. I told her, upon my return to the car, and we spent much of our lunch discussion talking about how need is everywhere and only through prayer, even short instantaneous prayers, is God able to completely impact for His glory.

It is not an accident that throughout Scripture, it is revealed that prayer was breath to Jesus. He never did anything without prayer, and surely, He would not have succeeded without it. He prayed when He was about to start His ministry, He prayed at the grave site of Lazarus, He prayed (or blessed) before turning two fish and five loaves into a meal for 5,000 men and an even greater number of women and children to eat, and He prayed, agonizingly, at the Garden of Gethsemane before going to the cross and accepting all of the sins of the world.

The Bible also recorded that He would wake up early in the morning to pray. He did it so often that His disciples noticed it. They also noticed that after Jesus prayed, His work was made easier, and He had more clarity. Hence the disciples approached Him and said, "Lord, teach us to pray" (Luke 11:1, NIV). This same Jesus said, "Men ought always to pray and not to faint" (Luke 18:1, KJV).

The prayers of Jesus enabled Him and His messages to have a great influence on the people He encountered. Whatever Jesus did, He tackled in the place of prayer, releasing the power of God to go ahead and make all crooked paths straight, so the way would be open for victories, favor, power, and influence.

How can you influence an adult who has already formed their own opinion about life? How can you persuade a full-grown man that his way of life is not God's way? You will need much more than oratorical power to accomplish this, and it will definitely take more than any knowledge you have obtained in school. It will take the power of God, and that power is always available to us through prayer.

*After they prayed, the place where they were meeting was shaken. And they were all filled with the Holy Spirit and spoke the word of God boldly.*
Acts 4:31, NIV

We see examples of people in the Bible who used the power of prayer to influence others; Nehemiah prayed, and he got favor from the king to rebuild the broken-down wall of Jerusalem. Esther and her people prayed and were able to influence the king to change the death sentence that was upon every Jew in his realm.

Prayer can turn situations around—it can melt the hearts of the hardened and make them subject to the Lordship of Jesus. It can open spiritually blind eyes, and it can pull down all strongholds and every imagination that rises up against the Lord. Prayer melts our hearts and redirects our lives. Through prayer, the impossible is accomplished.

### Jesus Obeys God

Jesus showed us how to live a life of obedience to God. From the beginning of His life on earth through His crucifixion and ascendance to Heaven, He never disobeyed God. Obedience is key to having close to us the presence of the Lord. Without the presence of God, we cannot achieve our purpose, nor can we realize the joy we are meant to experience. God is always close to people who are ready, at all times, to obey Him, and He is quick to bless those courageous enough to say *yes*.

When we obey God, our influence permeates. We saw

this happen in the Garden of Eden when Adam was still in tune with the plan and purpose of God for his life. Everything inside the garden obeyed him because he was obedient to God.

To influence people for God isn't about them obeying you or following you, but rather, it is for them to see God through you. I believe we know when we are in the presence of another Christian. I believe we are connected at a subconscious level to the degree that our spirits connect, or perhaps more accurately, the Holy Spirit living in us connects us as one—as brothers and sisters in Christ. Okay, let me explain. If the Holy Spirit lives in me and the Holy Spirit lives in you, aren't we connected? As God cannot coexist with sin or disobedience, then this connection only happens when we are living a holy and obedient life secured by grace. Jesus referred to the church as His "bride" in the singular.

*For where two or three are gathered together*
*in my name, there am I in the midst of them.*
Matthew 18:20, KJV

Serving God through obedience is an art, not a science. Most Christians ebb and flow; they struggle as much as they succeed. The key is simple: Focus on Jesus, and the Holy Spirit will show you the path to obedience.

Why is obedience important to a pleasing and fruitful service-filled life? I believe there is a natural order where goodness naturally follows God's presence. Think of the short but complicated story of Noah. Even after the fall of man, God was able to show us His goodness through the gathering of all the animals of the earth to the ark. There was no disturbance, no fighting, and no lion attacking sheep. Instead, through God, the animals and humans peacefully cohabitated in the ark, all because Noah obeyed God. When we obey our calling, the supernatural can occur.

## Calling Requires Influence

It is the presence of Christ in you that will make you shine for others to see—you cannot have Him in you and not influence those around you. He is the bright morning star and the Light of the world. The more you obey Him, the more His light shines on you.

*To them God has chosen to make known among*
*the Gentiles the glorious riches of this mystery,*
*which is Christ in you, the hope of glory.*
Colossians 1:27, NIV

### Jesus is Obedient

Jesus never allowed the flesh to rule or have any control over His life when He was on earth. Jesus understood fleshly nature and the problem this can cause in our life. It was completely natural for Him to discipline Himself to the Lord's will and put aside the deeds of the flesh. The flesh is our enemy; it carries the fallen nature of man, which often drives us from God. Little wonder the Bible says, when we are at home in the flesh, we are away from the Lord. Paul said, "For I know that good itself does not dwell in me, that is, in my sinful nature. For I have the desire to do what is good, but I cannot carry it out" (Romans 7:18, NIV).

Our service reflects a more attractive life to those we serve. Even to the worst offenders—the people we influence are those who have given their lives to all kinds of misdirection. By showing God's love in tangible ways, we reveal the love and luster not found in the carnal life.

*The acts of the flesh are obvious: sexual immorality,*
*impurity and debauchery; idolatry and witchcraft;*
*hatred, discord, jealousy, fits of rage, selfish ambition,*
*dissensions, factions and envy; drunkenness, orgies,*

*and the like. I warn you, as I did before, that those who live like this will not inherit the kingdom of God.*
Galatians 5:19-21, NIV

In my life, the "big ones" outlined in Galatians 5, don't seem to be my biggest temptations or sources of disobedience. Self-reliance and financial security are what separate me most from God. I was talking to a very close friend about praying for our businesses and the dip we are both experiencing, which is really testing our fiscal health. He hit the nail on the head when he gave me this truth: When we are praying for God to take the financial pressure away, when we ask for the burden to be lifted, and when we wrestle with God about His allowing the burden to consume us, what we are really praying for is for God to relieve our burden to be reliant on Him. Let me repeat—when we pray for God to fix our security problems, be they financial or anything else, this denies His being our source of security. What we are really praying is, "God, I have control of this, and you've got control of the rest." My friend made it clear to me, "There is no way God is going to honor that prayer; no way!" That was a reality check for me—a real revelation for me to consider.

I wish I could tell you that with that realization came victory, but, on the contrary, the desire for financial self-reliance is a continued struggle and area of lack of obedience for me. My flesh is afraid of letting go to be completely reliant on God's provision. So, I don't get in real trouble here, I do believe stock portfolios and 401(k)'s are ways for God to provide for us and show His care for us. I think the lesson for me has been that it is not money that is evil, but the love of money, or in my case, the self-reliance money perpetuates. That is at the core of my struggle.

For us to succeed at serving people who are entangled, we must be free from the entanglement ourselves. By the power of the Holy Spirit, we can be strong against the works of the flesh and be free to live for God. Only through reliance on the Holy Spirit can we overcome ourselves.

*Therefore, there is now no condemnation for those who are in Christ Jesus, because through Christ Jesus the law of the Spirit who gives life has set you free from the law of sin and death. For what the law was powerless to do because it was weakened by the flesh, God did by sending his own Son in the likeness of sinful flesh to be a sin offering. And so he condemned sin in the flesh, in order that the righteous requirement of the law might be fully met in us, who do not live according to the flesh but according to the Spirit.*
Romans 8:1-4, NIV

**Jesus is Anointed**

Without the power of God, we can not influence others. This is the reason why Jesus told His disciples not to rush to do the great commission but to tarry in Jerusalem until they received the power from the Holy Spirit. Then, they could begin to manifest the saving message of Jesus in the world.

When the power of God is evident, influencing others becomes easy. Through the Holy Spirit, hearts are softened and made available. The Bible says, “In the day of His power His people shall be willing” (Psalm 103, KJV). No one can resist God—the Bible says all power belongs to Him, hence He is unstoppable.

*How God anointed Jesus of Nazareth with the Holy Spirit and power, and how he went around doing good and healing all who were under the power of the*

*devil, because God was with him.*
Acts 10:38, NLT

With God's anointing, Jesus was able to cast out demons, heal the sick, deliver the oppressed, raise the dead, preach the gospel . . . on and on. All of this greatly influenced those He encountered. And to think He only had three years of ministry to do the work is astonishing.

Astonishing anointings were not just meant for Jesus. Paul's anointing by Jesus is perhaps the most powerful ministerial anointing in history. Paul's radical life transformation led this simple tentmaker to create the first Christian Church and draw others to Christ.

When we are anointed, we are able to reach people we never thought we could. In 2007, being anointed became very real to me. I was a sales executive for a large business consulting firm for about five years, and by then, I was well-known in the company and respected by my coworkers and customers. I never let my faith be a mystery, nor was I shy about my life. That summer, my wife, Valerie, and I took a huge step and decided we were going to go to Kenya for a Saddleback Church mission trip. This meant taking our twelve and fourteen-year-old daughters as well. It was a miracle, to me, the way I was treated after returning to work. Whenever anybody takes a month off work, people notice, and contrary to how you think I might have been treated upon my return, it was amazing to me what happened. Coworkers who would have never thought of speaking about church or spiritual things in the workplace opened up and felt free to explore my motivations for going and asked questions about my experience while I was there. It was truly a foreign thing to most I spoke with, to consider dropping everything to take on church work in Africa.

In our decision and sacrifice, Valerie and I made sure we were bathed in prayer and anointed for the trip. That anointment was made clear, both while in Africa and when we returned. This trip provided new opportunities for connection and transparency with people.. I learned about the faith and testimony of many, and, the most amazing thing, I was able to share why a life of service is so important to me. I was able to freely understand God's love and Jesus' saving message.

Throughout history, we see men like Billy Graham, Charles Finney, William Wilberforce, Smith Wigglesworth, Charles Spurgeon, Jonathan Edward, and other of God's Generals doing amazing things for God, while ushering in great revivals of modern times, all on the platform of the power of God's anointing.

The anointing is still available for our generation. The Bible says, "For everyone who asks, receives. Anyone who seeks, finds. If only you will knock, the door will open." (Matthew 7:8, TLB).

**Jesus Loves All**

God is love. Jesus loved all, including those who seemed unlovable. He never discriminated. When the woman who was caught in adultery was brought to Him, her accusers thought the Great Master would immediately condemn her to death, but Jesus showed love by making the accusers aware that they were not better than her. He did the same for Zacchaeus the tax collector, for the adulterous woman who poured oil on His feet and wiped them with her hair, for Mary Magdalene, from whom He cast out seven demons, and countless other sinners.

There is no other thing that can influence others faster than love. When we show love to others, they are more likely to respond positively to whatever we are bringing before them. As I see it, the world expects us to tolerate each other, but God expects us to love each other. We need to preach God's message with love, knowing full well we were once in need of grace, and it is the same love of God that made salvation available to us.

Love can make you tolerate the most abominable person, to see the person as a potential child of God, and then, use all heavenly resources obtained, through prayer, to pull the person out of the fruitless life they are living. Fruitlessness can be deceiving—even the most successful people we know are eternally fruitless without God. Love will make you see the good side of every person, no matter how difficult it may be to find. Love will make you speak positively and encourage good things for them. Indeed, you can influence others and bring them to God with love.

**Jesus is Passionate**

Our Lord has a great, unquenchable passion for lost souls. Throughout His ministry, Jesus looked for seekers everywhere so He could minister to them. He knew God did not originally create anyone to be bad and that every evil work we see today is a result of the fall of man. He was ready to lay down His life for the salvation of all souls, and He actually did it without holding anything back.

Around us are people who are emotionally disturbed, neglected, frustrated with life, mentally imbalanced, and who have been abused in all ways you can imagine. They need help, but they will not come on their own. We must reach out and create an atmosphere of love that will allow seekers to see the everlasting life Jesus offers them.

**Jesus is Holy**

Our Lord lived a holy life while on earth. So holy was He, that when He was about to be crucified, they could not find anyone to come forward to utter any evil or crime He had committed. The holiness of Jesus influenced others because they could see it in Him, and they could easily differentiate it from the hypocrisy of the Pharisees.

Understanding that everybody around is watching us proves critical to understanding the need to live a holy life. If we express our faith to our coworkers but hit the topless bar while attending a convention, are we demonstrating a life well-lived in Christ? If we yell and scream at our children over spilled milk, are we showing our children composure and self-control? If we shout at a referee for a bad call at a ball game, are we acting holy? Living a holy life is as much reactive as it is proactive. The world is looking for a person who can live the kind of life the Bible teaches. People want to see practical holiness in this generation of no fine line or real truth, just shades of gray. We can be that person who shows them what God's holiness is. They actually want to know whether it is possible, and many of them want to emulate it, once they see it in a person.

*I will not say much more to you, for the prince of this world is coming. He has no hold over me.*
John 14:30, NIV

### The Wrong Type of Influence

At this point, I would be remiss if I didn't call out the contrary. Everybody, in one way or the other, influences others around them, whether actively or passively; whatever we do touches others and can make them act. I tell my girls all of the time—especially in the digital age— someone or something is watching us all of the time: online, surveillance cameras, or in a crowd with cell phone cameras. The world is watching and judging God's people. Missteps or improper actions can lead others astray and cause them to reject Christ altogether.

During her time as an athlete at Baylor University, my oldest daughter, Alecia, had a social footprint of over 15,000 followers. As her father, it was very interesting watching her navigate that responsibility. Over the course of those few years, we had more than a few conversations about the responsibility she had to always remember that in every post, she had to remember who she was, who she represented, and what her purpose was. I am proud to say that with only a few missteps, Alecia handled the responsibility with composure and grace.

Whatever we Christians do or say that could point others away from Christ is a missed opportunity for the Holy Spirit's influence. We must avoid these instances. Know that you are not expected to live for yourselves alone, but you are to work towards helping others see the person of Christ in your life. Anything that is evil will make us collaborators with sinners and will easily pass a wrong message to others.

*Reject every kind of evil.*
I Thessalonians 5:22, NIV

God's influence is not for wealth or fame. If our motive for influencing others is to get the approval of men or to gain an advantage over others, then we are not representing God. If we are popular and accepted through ill gain here on earth, and have lost our first love in faith, then our acclaim, esteem, or favor is all for nothing. Recognition in heaven and representing God is where our great prize can be found.

We have all heard the sayings, "Fame is fleeting," and "Everyone gets their five minutes of fame." In our culture, the saddest among us seem to be those who appear to "have it all." Having lived most of my life in southern California's culture, it's always "mystifying" (pun intended) that the Hollywood crowd chases its tail trying to find "spiritual" enlightenment but never really seems to. I wish I had a nickel for every actor who found Maharaj Ji this, or self-help Guru that. Many of us have the God of the universe introduced to us by our parents and Sunday school teachers from the time we are children, yet we chase rainbows halfway around the world. I don't get it!

### Jesus Guides and Develops Leaders

By our calling, we are leaders. This is not because we are trained as managers by the best business schools, or because we attended the most rigorous military training, or use our personal wealth, but because we have access to God directly. One of the things that man has sought, throughout time, is access to a supreme being who will guide him into the future. We, who are Christ followers, already have the Creator of Heaven and Earth as our Lord and Savior, hence we are secure.

The Spirit of God in us helps us understand what to do in times when we are at a loss in a difficult circumstance. I was really at a loss recently when I was asked for some marital advice from a friend. I didn't know what to say, so I immediately prayed for the Holy Spirit to use me through some sage wisdom. I certainly have no expertise in marital counseling except to have successfully been married to Valerie for almost thirty-nine years. Valerie once asked me why I round up when telling others how long we have been married. I simply said, "It feels longer," and she responded with, "Yaa—it does!" Ouch! She got me, but it really does, and in a good way. I only have vague memories of my life before her and feel most everything important in my life has happened with her, and that was the point. Through marriage, we have grown into one. When she hurts, I hurt. What makes her happy, makes me happy. Where she goes, I go. I really did not know how to respond to the questions other than to say marriage is a gift, and it is what we make it. If God says it's good, who are we to make it bad?

## Whose Job is it Anyway?

Good and bad are relative to how we respond to circumstances. We choose how we respond, with God or without. That is why Jesus called us the salt of the earth. God, in us, brings out the sweetness that makes a difference in people's lives. My wife, Valerie, would argue that salt on watermelon makes it taste sweeter and I look at her like she's crazy. Clearly, the salt on watermelon enhances its flavor in the same way we, as believers, enrich the lives of others.

Leadership is all about influence, and in this case, we are to influence people to accept the Lordship of Christ. The Apostle Paul said He made himself all things to all men so He could save as many as possible. To the Jews He became a Jew; to the Gentiles, He became a Gentile. Meeting people where they are is critical to encouraging a heart receptive to the Gospel.

Know that it is good to lead for and serve God. He is the best employer and the only reward, but working for God, without His power, can be frustrating. Seek the face of God for power: power to influence others and power to live a victorious Christian life, full of God's favor and blessing others. The closer we are to God, the easier it is to influence others in love. We must first allow God to influence us so we can influence others in His name.

## FIVE

# Yes - "YOUR" CALLING!

Don't be surprised to hear this: You have been called by God to do a specific task for a specific purpose, which explains the reason why you are here. It explains why we are on the Earth at this time, born of our parents, in the town in which we currently reside, working the job we currently have, with the spouse we have been gifted, and with the children who have been placed in our charge. You might say, "I am not a religious person, nor am I a clergyman, a preacher, or a missionary. Why am I being called by God to be used for his purpose?"

The truth is, most people don't know what they have been created for or what their purpose is. Soul searching is as old as the hills. Amazon is riddled with self-help and self-identity books, and throughout modern times, more than our share of charlatans and gurus have created huge followings, preying on people seeking to find themselves. Most people search and simply follow the first shiny idea that appeals to them most. Culture today provides norms that drive the definition of success or failure. People just seem to follow the path of least resistance to making a living by trying to achieve or getting as close to "success" as possible. It is no wonder most are living paycheck to paycheck, from weekend to weekend, or vacation to vacation. Our lives have become frustrating because we have defined success with popularity or dollar signs rather than service and meaningful long-term human impact.

## Whose Job is it Anyway?

I must admit, I am just as guilty as the next guy when it comes to chasing the almighty dollar. I have always viewed my time as a banana, and every hour that I worked and did not get paid or did not make as much money as I could have, it was as if the banana had browned and spoiled. It became unsellable, rotten, and lost forever. Aside from my time as a military officer in the Air Force, I have never really worked for or seen my job as a sense of service or mission. My time in aviation management and technology was all about making as much money as I possibly could.

I am a businessman. We are judged by sales, profit and loss, wealth creation, growth, business expansion, and job creation. We outsell or out-maneuver the competition. Is any of that wrong? I don't believe it is. Throughout the Bible, business success is seen as a blessing from God to many of those who were chosen by God to do His purpose. But, here is where I have missed it for most of my career and most of my life: the real words to focus on are not success, growth, or profit. The word is "blessing." If we see our life's work as our mission and the fulfillment of our purpose, the fruits of our labor take on a whole new meaning. They are naturally defined as blessings. If I see my business success or my successful sale of the latest technology as a blessing to others, it becomes much more important to me and to who I am. As a pilot, if I view flying a trip from New York to London, not as the moving of a machine from one place to another, but as a vessel that is re-uniting families and friends, facilitating a big business deal, or a bridge bringing about stronger relationships, it becomes very easy to see my work as a blessing and a calling.

In addition, in whatever profession or career we have chosen, there is a specific assignment we have from God that will go with what we are doing. In other words, if we see our work as the fulfillment of our purpose, we are all bi-vocational, some even multi-vocational. This is the reason why we will often discover that we are gifted in more than one area; we have the ability to do things that are worthwhile in more than one area of life.

*Now there are varieties of gifts, but the same Spirit; and there are varieties of service, but the same Lord; and there are varieties of activities, but it is the same God who empowers them all in everyone.*
1 Corinthians 12:4-6, ESV

Spiritual gifts are God's tools for us to leverage for His glory, to fulfill His purposes, and for our purpose and well-being. God wants to use us in those particular areas where we have been specifically and spiritually gifted.

Our gifts, talents, and endowments are not given to us for our profit alone; their purpose is much more than that. If all we are thinking about is how to enrich ourselves and our families with our gifts, we are missing a lot. In fact, much of what sets us apart as Christians is our spiritual gifts. Unfortunately, through laziness, lack of interest, or simple apathy, many Christians will never harness the full potential of those gifts. Every gift is given for the purpose of serving God, and until they are directed toward such, they will not fully benefit us or God.

**Our Source of Joy**

Today, a lack of fulfillment and depression have reached epidemic proportions. Even in the Christian world, lack of joy and well-being is a big issue. Joy has become a foreign concept for most. Though written about and taught, it is rarely experienced. Why is it that people reach for alcohol or substances to achieve a sense of joy or well-being? I believe it is in large part due to trading in our sense of mission and purpose for the stress of chasing the almighty dollar. Only when we reach our purpose, gifted by our Creator, will we achieve our joy and well-being.

Our family has been faced with the biggest battle of our life—the dreaded "C" word: Cancer. My wife Valerie has breast cancer. What was first thought to be very early detection, with a routine prescription of radiation therapy, has exploded into the realization that the cancer is much faster moving and invasive than originally thought, with the subsequent need to move her to the City of Hope to keep her alive. Recently, the days have been dark and would be unbearable without our faith. This is especially true for her, as the treatment has advanced to a recipe of chemotherapy drugs including Adriamycin, the "Red Devil," a derivative of mustard gas.

The tests of life can be painful, and Christians are not immune to any of the world's flaws. The refiner's fire can be especially important for people of faith, as God prepares and protects us in preparation for services to Him. I am the first to admit: faith and desire to act on my calling are weak, seemingly nonexistent, as Valerie is in a fight for her life, and I endure, sitting on the sideline, unable to help. I am clinging to my faith that our prayers are sufficient and our God is great. We are all subject to life's realities, and in my case, it's a chore right now to practice what I preach. It seems there are more dark days right now than joy, but we cling to the fact that the love of Jesus carries us through the valley of darkness.

*Vindicate me, my God, and plead my cause*
*against an unfaithful nation.*
*Rescue me from those who are*
*deceitful and wicked.*
*You are God my stronghold.*
*Why have you rejected me?*
*Why must I go about mourning,*
*oppressed by the enemy?*

## Yes - "YOUR" CALLING!

*Send me your light and your faithful care,*
*let them lead me;*
*let them bring me to your holy mountain,*
*to the place where you dwell.*
*Then I will go to the altar of God,*
*to God, my joy and my delight.*
*I will praise you with the lyre,*
*O God, my God.*
*Why, my soul, are you downcast?*
*Why so disturbed within me?*
*Put your hope in God,*
*for I will yet praise him,*
*my Savior and my God.*
Psalm 43, NIV

The truth is, life's pressures aren't typically big events that explode in our path like cancer; they are almost always a series of small obstacles, building and building that derail us. How do we get from where we are to where God is taking us? Let's face it; we have real demands that, in most cases, are virtually impossible to escape—a lifestyle, a mortgage on our home, at least one car payment or two, dance class for our daughters, and a new pair of cleats for our sons. But, through relying on Jesus as our source, we realize there can be joy in even the hard parts of life.

God is an all-knowing God. He doesn't make mistakes in choosing people for His work. When God enlightens the eyes of our understanding, the eyes of our hearts, we will be able to see the invisible and hear the inaudible, and we will become fulfilled in life, as God intended it. God made us all, and He knows what we are made of, including our limitations, our failings, and our fears. He gives us what He knows we need to live, to function, and to succeed for Him. He blesses us!

## Whose Job is it Anyway?

*And we know that in all things God works for the good of those who love him, who have been called according to his purpose. For those God foreknew he also predestined to be conformed to the image of his Son, that he might be the firstborn among many brothers and sisters. And those he predestined, he also called; those he called, he also justified; those he justified, he also glorified.*
Romans 8:28-30, NIV

God knows us more than we know ourselves. He knew us when we entered our mother's womb. He can recount every experience we went through when we were growing up and before we fully recognized who we are. He knows every little bit about our lives. He has chosen for us what will give us a fulfilling life, and He knows the path to joy.

*You will show me the path of life;*
*In Your presence is fullness of joy;*
*At Your right hand are pleasures forevermore.*
Psalm 16:11, NKJV

Until we fully understand the concept of our purpose being a core element to who we are, it will be impossible to lead a fulfilled and productive life.

I am more and more convinced we have an internal barometer, a gauge in our soul, that tells us if we are in tune with our mission and our purpose and whether or not we are in sync with God's plan for our lives. It is also clear to me that fame, fortune, or success have no bearing on what the internal gauge is reading. I said it earlier, but it bears repeating: the rich and famous among us can be sad, frustrated, and unfulfilled, and the poor can be the happiest people we will ever know. I experienced this firsthand while visiting downright destitute villages in Kenya. Villagers would greet us with amazing joy and happiness. As we learned of the tragedy and brokenness in their lives, it was revealed they had completely surrendered to God, and with that surrender, came joy and peace. A real sense of sadness and joy, at the same time, came over me when I realized it was them ministering to me, not the other way around.

We need to discover who we are and what we are here for if we want to truly be joyful. Self-discovery is actually the foundation of success in life and the basis for understanding our purpose. We cannot receive this revelation from prestigious colleges and universities or even through the academic rigors of a fine seminary. No matter how deep our soul-searching or the academics take us, they are too far from reality. Only God can open our eyes to discover this truth that will set our minds and feet on the right path. Our strength is in our purpose.

The Apostle Paul knew the importance of receiving this revelation from God. The following is a prayer pattern we find Paul praying for the Christians of his time:

*I pray that the eyes of your heart may be enlightened in order that you may know the hope to which he has called you, the riches of his glorious inheritance in his holy people, and his incomparably great power for us who believe. That power is the same as the mighty strength he exerted when he raised Christ from the dead and seated him at his right hand in the heavenly realms . . .*
Ephesians 1:18-20, NIV

## SIX

# A "Life" Calling

God has the ability to completely relate our calling to us. God reveals all we need to know about our area of calling. He did the same for the saints in the Bible: Moses reluctantly lead the Israelites out of bondage, Joshua was the successor to Moses leading the Israelites out of Egypt, Jeremiah was chosen to reveal God's awesome promise that however bleak, He is always in control, Samuel guided the kings to remain committed to God's source and provision, Daniel lead through his steadfast witness and commitment to God, forsaking all temptation and speaking prophetically God's promises, just to name a few. If God has called us, He will surely speak to us and show us what our calling entails, but that can only be possible if we are close enough to hear Him. Close enough means leaning into the Holy Spirit's presence in us. Honestly, it took me too long to admit the Holy Spirit was already ever-present in my life. At first I prayed for the "Holy Spirit to come to me or be with me", not realizing the power of the Holy Spirit entered the instant I accepted Christ as my savior. The Holy Spirit is ever present with us and will forever be.

Here's a word of caution: Many of us seeking a calling or feeling the tug of a calling, automatically gravitate to a radical life change or feel a need to reinvent ourselves into somebody different. For some, that will be necessary. However, for the vast majority of us, to live our calling means we simply must transform our perspective of who and what we are living for and who and what we serve.

Let's take some time and see what God has said about our calling, as stated in the Bible, the only book approved by God to guide us into the glorious life He chose for us, even before the foundation of the world.

**Our Calling is a Gift From God**

This is the first thing we need to know about God's calling: It is a gift. Nobody on earth deserves to be called by God. We are not prepared for nor do we really deserve to be considered as workers in the Lord's vineyard. But, God wants many children. It was His plan, since Adam, to fellowship with us. The grace brought through Jesus was necessary because He wants us to share in His eternal glory and be part of what He is doing on Earth as well as in Heaven.

*God, by His grace through Christ, has*
*called you to become his people.*
Galatians 1:6a, NCV

The calling of God is not by educational attainment, moral justification, human endeavors, or whatever good thing we might consider as a qualification for a higher calling in life. The standard of God's assignments far supersedes what all human efforts and understanding can aspire to. Our calling is far too big for us to fulfill on our own. Our gift is free and pre-ordained, but we must say *yes*, then let God be God.

This concept has been tough for me to grasp; it's counter-cultural for me. As pilots, we earn our wings through licenses, ratings, and performance, first as Private Pilots, then as Commercial Pilots, and finally as Airline Transport Pilots. We start with small single-engine planes, then work our way up to twin-engine props, turbo props, small jets, big jets, and even supersonic jets. It is always about performance! God has other plans. In His world, it's about saying *yes*!

One of the biggest lessons I understand from the Biblical illustration of the Sadducees is their arrogance. They held a mindset that we become holy because of what we do, the sacrifices we make, and how wise we are. They missed it altogether, and Jesus made it clear for us to see. Nobody can boast about their calling because it is not what we have been able to attain or what we have done through our human effort. It is our privilege for God to call us and gift us our unique purpose and calling.

*He has saved us and called us to a holy*
*life – not because of anything we have done*
*but because of his own purpose and grace.*
2 Timothy 1:9, NIV

God's reason for calling us is purely because of His purpose for our lives—the reason He created us and sent us into this world. As we see from the words of Jeremiah, His purpose for us was preordained before we were born.

*Before I formed you in the womb I knew you,*
*And before you were born I consecrated you;*
*I have appointed you a prophet to the nations.*
Jeremiah 1:5, NASB

**We are Called for God's Purpose**

God's calling on our life is for His purpose, a purpose only He knows of and one that He will reveal to us in His own time. As I discuss throughout these chapters, God, more times than not, uses people who man would never see as the logical choice. I believe God uses people who are less capable or less acceptable in man's eyes, so when His will is carried out, it is without question the work of God and not from the capabilities of he or she who accomplished the work. In the story of Samuel, someone well-built and good-looking like Eliab, the eldest brother of David, was more likely to be king. Had he not been instructed by God, and even if David had been present at the gathering of the brothers, Samuel would never have picked him as king. Through Samuel's eyes, David was not tall enough, not strong enough, or even pretty enough to be king. God saw him differently. He saw David through his calling.

I see this unfold in business all of the time. As a business leader, I organize and plan around team dynamics, experience, and the skill sets of my employees. I am constantly surprised at who steps up and makes it happen and who disappoints in the end. One very surprising example occurred many years ago when I was working with my business partner, hiring and setting expectations for a team we were putting at a customer site in Europe. This leadership plan was very important to us and to the future success of our company; success with this assignment would put our small aerospace company on the world stage.

As an aerospace company working on military projects, we gravitated to hiring former service members. Because of the sensitivity and technical complexity of our work, we hired former senior officers almost exclusively. What happened with the team several months in really surprised me. After a careful selection process and vetting of the team, the one person who stepped up as the trusted and effective leader was the former enlisted tanker boom operator, and the biggest disappointment was the former full bird colonel fighter pilot who we thought was the natural leadership fit. The person who achieved the least in military service was significantly more gifted in leadership than the former officer who led hundreds and perhaps thousands of airmen throughout their military service. To this day, I still cringe when I think about the assumptions we made. How could we have been so wrong as we hired the team?

As He did with David, God can use seemingly average people to carry out His plan. He usually surprises us with who He calls and what He calls us to. Often, people called by God seem to be unqualified, at least when we look at them from our human perspective.

Moses was a fugitive and a man of slow speech, Peter was uneducated and a mere fisherman, and Paul was the chief persecutor of the church God wanted Him to lead. How could God go for such people, despite their beginnings? Because He had already ordained them for His calling, and what they were doing at the time had no bearing on what they were meant to do for God. Where we are, currently, has nothing to do with whether we will be successful at God's assignment for us once we accept our calling.

Whatever we are doing now, no matter how far away from God we may be or inept we may feel, our reluctance means nothing to God. If the maker of heaven and earth has ordained us for a specific task, He knows how to make us successful at it. The truth is, we are probably already there; we just need to be willing to say *yes*.

### Your Calling Was Chosen and Cemented Before You Were Born

*Yet, before the twins were born or had done anything good or bad—in order that God's purpose in election might stand: not by works but by him who calls—she was told, "The older will serve the younger."*
Romans 9:11-12, NIV

God's calling is not an afterthought; it is not a new

strategy to correct a mistake that has been made by someone else or redrawn based on who will or will not act. God had His entire plan laid down before the foundation of the world, and we are included in that plan. The role that every individual will play in the plan is already known by God, and in His omnipotence, His work is done. Our role in God's plan is that of actors only appearing to play as the script was written.

*Before I shaped you in the womb I knew all about you,*
*before you saw the light of day I had holy plans for you.*
Jeremiah 1:5, MSG

How do we feel when we hear the CEO of our company has plans for us, the mentor we greatly respect has plans for us, or even the President of our country has plans for us? Of course, we are joyful at the opportunity, and we are happy at the thought of being selected, trusted, and respected. The thought that the CEO, our mentor, or even the President could call us causes us to feel humbled to be considered for such favor. Should we not feel the same joy and fulfillment from being called by the Creator of the universe? Should we not have the same ambition to serve and please God?

The notion that God has called me to do His work is a big deal! I am not sure this concept is easy to grasp. In most cases, I act in obedience and not out of honor. I serve because I am led to but not with the realization I am commissioned from on high. To be called and to fulfill our calling is something to grasp with an eternal perspective. To act on our calling is to say *yes* to the President of Presidents and King of Kings. Acting on our calling translates into influencing eternity for God's will. It's a really BIG deal!

Before we were born, God already knew what He wanted to do with our lives. He already knew why He was sending us into the world. Everything about our lives is transparent to God, and our paths are set for His purpose. Now, do we stray from that path? Yes; absolutely, and sometimes in really big ways. Our sinful nature is sometimes a very powerful force pulling us in the wrong direction. The farther away we stray from God, the more powerful our sinful nature becomes. Through acts of free will, we can blow it big time and hurt many people in the process. No journey astray is too far gone though. God always provides us with a path back to His will and to our purpose. As a jet pilot, I have done some really dangerous things in airplanes. However, the one thing I always knew was if things went wrong, if something malfunctioned, or even if I made a bad decision resulting in imminent doom, I had my ejection seat and parachute to save me. We need to understand that even when we have really blown it, God provides us with an ejection seat and a parachute.

At Saddleback Church, we have a great example of one of God's paths home. Celebrate Recovery is a life-changing ministry where over two million people have steered away from life's addictions and towards God's calling for their lives. Much like Alcoholics Anonymous, Celebrate Recovery provides a plan for healing and detoxification. Unlike AA and other similar programs, Celebrate Recovery includes the reality that we cannot be fully healed or reach a complete life until we understand that our strength comes from God, through Jesus Christ, and that understanding our calling and our purpose is necessary for healing and leading a whole life. Equally miraculous is the blessing of having formerly broken people leading the process of healing for new entrants in the program. The Founder of Celebrate Recovery, John Baker, was an alcoholic, transformed by Christ, and acting on his calling as a lay minister at Saddleback. John was led to author the manuscript for *Celebrate* and sent it to Pastor Rick seeking support. In his typical fashion, Pastor Rick said, "If God says go with it, then go with it, and we'll support you." Statistically, Celebrate Recovery is by far the most successful program of its type and for good reason. When we know who we are and whose we are, our paths will be straight.

Our calling can manifest itself in many places: sometimes from life experience, sometimes from intervention, and sometimes from simple brokenness. It is often hard for us to be willing to accept where God's path takes us, and that's okay; God knows every path is as He designed. Conversely, many know they were called from birth to do God's heavy lifting. As I wrote these thoughts, I was in the End of Life Care Unit at the OU Health Science Presbyterian Hospital in Oklahoma City. My eighty-nine-year-old mother was on her way to meet our Lord, and for the last few days, I was honored with the company of the hospital's end-of-life specialists. The nurses and doctors are truly living their calling, whether they know it or not.

Our nurse, appropriately named Grace, was a testament to someone who is completely aware of and working through her calling. During our twelve-hour shift with Grace, we talked about many experiences she has had during her fifteen years as a hospice nurse, and perhaps, her most revealing comment was her complete understanding that her work is exactly why God put her on earth. Grace claimed, "This job is precisely why I was born." Grace was compelling in her conviction that the death process is less about loss and more about a beautiful transition to eternity. It was clear to me that Grace is not a care nurse for death, but she is called to be a midwife delivering children to Heaven.

As with the birth process, there is a similar process in death. There is a time of pain, stress, and uncertainty, but at the end of the process, there is a new life in Christ—an eternal life full of happiness, comfort, and joy in the presence of God. Think of the birth process. The baby is comfortably surrounded by amniotic fluid, with the umbilical cord providing nourishment for healthy growth in a worry-free existence.

## A "Life" Calling

Nine months into the safe, warm, and growing life of the baby, there are labor pains and contractions. What happens next is a removal from his or her current reality and a birth into a world of bright lights and loud noises. Ponder this for a moment: with all of the wonder and experience ahead of the newborn baby, consider what we have ahead as we make the transition to heaven and eternal life with God. The death of our physical body stows fear and uncertainty for most, but can you imagine the glory and wonder that awaits us in heaven? I thank God for Grace and her calling. Her willingness to do a very hard job for God has meant peace and comfort for countless numbers who make the transition to Heaven's eternity.

*But even before I was born, God chose me*
*and called me by his marvelous grace.*
Galatians 1:15, NLT

The Apostle Paul, author of the book of Galatians, calls it an undeserved mercy for the Almighty God to think upon him and choose him for his specific assignment. God's perfect timing worked with Paul's birth and life. The good, the bad, and the ugly came together to fulfill God's plan. There were others who could have done the job, but Paul was called to it. It was his as ordained by God for His purpose. It is an undeserved mercy indeed, considering the fact that we are all sinners, and some even enemies of God's will. Yet, God can still consider us to be useful for His glorious assignments. No wonder He is called the merciful God.

## SEVEN

# Sins and Mistakes

*I thank Christ Jesus our Lord, who has given me strength, that he considered me trustworthy, appointing me to his service. Even though I was once a blasphemer and a persecutor and a violent man, I was shown mercy because I acted in ignorance and unbelief. The grace of our Lord was poured out on me abundantly, along with the faith and love that are in Christ Jesus.*
1 Timothy 1:12-14, NIV

A very difficult thing for most people is seeing themselves the way God sees them—through the eyes of Jesus and not their own. We see imperfection, but God sees perfection through the grace of Christ's sacrifice. God sees us as desirable and perfect for His will because we are His creation. In the same way a mother sees for her child, God sees us for what we will be, not what we are or what we have done. We should not look at ourselves as sinners too dirty to be used by God but as His creation made for His purpose. Our God cannot coexist with evil or sin, but routinely, God uses our past mistakes for His purpose. For most, this is a shocking reality, but I believe God wants us to see it as liberating.

As we see ourselves through the lens of our flaws, it is equally as difficult to look at others without judgment. We see decisions people have made, but God sees His calling on their lives and His perfect purpose according to His plan. We need to be careful when looking at others we have known in the past. They may have lived their lives so badly that we can hardly see them worthy of an earthly, not to mention a Heavenly appointment, but God will surprise us with His appointments.

If God is marking iniquity, then no man can stand up to the measure against them, and no man can escape the judgment of our sinful life. We are born into sin, hence all of us are sinners, originally. Sin is a part of our nature through free will; there is nothing we can do on our own that can deliver us from that. But God is looking beyond our flaws. God decided that if we were to be free to love Him, we also needed to be free to chart our own paths, both good and bad. God allows us to go full-length into the sins that overcome us; then, at the right time, He knows when we are ready to accept our calling and live for our purpose. Only when we seek His life jacket or reach for the ejection seat handle, will He intervene. God rescues us only when we allow ourselves to be rescued. We may be the worst sinners on Earth today, but that does not change anything about the plan of God. He can still use us all the same, according to His will. I can imagine in the time and place when Paul realized his calling and acted on it, others were quick to say, "Look at him; if he can be called of God, I can be called of God as well." Paul was a testament to God's power at work.

Scripture is clear throughout, the saving grace of Jesus Christ is for every person on earth. Your place of birth and the color of your skin are already determined. But the decisions of your past are just that, in your past. Accepting Jesus as your Lord and Savior means you are cleansed in His blood and made new through His ultimate sacrifice. It is very, very important to understand that our past doesn't have anything to do with how God will use us.

*From that city many of the Samaritans believed*

*in Him because of the word of the woman who testified, "He told me all the things that I have done."*
John 4:39, NASB

Also compelling is what happened at Sychar, a territory of Samaria where a woman who had lived with five men encountered Jesus. As outlined in John 4, this woman reveals herself as a repeat adultress and someone who is socially living in a careless and sinful manner.

*He said to her, "Go, call your husband and come here." The woman answered and said, "I have no husband." Jesus said to her, "You have correctly said, 'I have no husband'; for you have had five husbands, and the one whom you now have is not your husband; this which you have said is true."*
John 4:16-18, NASB

When she told other people her testimony, they surrendered their lives to Christ, easily. It was clear to the Samaritans that if God could reach perhaps the most offensive sinner amongst them, they, too, could know God and be called by Him.

Even though one could say that Moses was past his prime in life, he was able to do God's will. He was already old (about eighty years of age) when he was wanted for murder in Egypt. He ran away from the place God wanted to use him. One would think he had successfully closed all of the avenues through which God could use him, but despite all of Moses' flaws and social stains, God did not go for a replacement. He used Moses to set His people free according to His plan and Moses' calling. What a Mighty God!

As far as God is concerned, our sin is nothing. The blood of Jesus is adequate to take care of all sin; all we need to do is wash ourselves in the blood and become clean, ready for the Master's use. The deeper we have been in sin, the more we will be able to appreciate the goodness of God after He rescues us from its grip.

Another thing we must realize is there is no plan B with God. His plans are so perfect that nothing in the whole of eternity can make Him change or update them. Omnipotence has its privilege—God sees all, knows all, and certainly facilitates whatever role He has given us to play. We are the best person for it; not because of what we have done but because our Creator has already ordained and equipped us for that role, even if we can not see anything that demonstrates ordained qualifications in ourselves.

When Moses finally stood before God to be sent to Egypt, his issue with stammering came to light. Consider this: How can a person who struggles with a stutter be sent for such a very important *speaking* assignment? Of course, Moses complained and expressed his lack of confidence, but God asked him, "Who made the mouth?" Prior to God's call, the life of Moses was turning to that of a useless man who failed to lay hold of any good achievement, all because he was far away from the place of his purpose. He was already living at the backside of the mountain and would have died there if God had not gone to fetch him.

*And Moses said unto the Lord, "O my Lord, I am not eloquent, neither heretofore nor since Thou hast spoken unto Thy servant; but I am slow of speech and of a slow tongue." 11 And the Lord said unto him, "Who hath made man's mouth? Or who maketh the dumb or deaf, or the seeing or the blind? Have not I, the Lord?" 12 "Now therefore go, and I will be with thy mouth and teach thee what thou shalt say."*
Exodus 4:10-12, 21st Century King James Version

No matter how well *we* feel we may fit into a role, it takes God to qualify us. Only if we are acting out of our calling will we be effective. What Moses could not achieve, when he was a younger man charting his own path, was made easy when he accepted his calling. Even the influence on the throne of Egypt was handed to him because it was God's will. When Moses led through his calling, his work was good, and he had a good reputation among the people. God called Moses at eighty years old, while he was still a fugitive of Egypt. This truly goes to show that, with God, nothing is impossible. Neither our age nor our circumstances can diminish our impact for His kingdom.

We cannot deviate from the purpose of God and live a fulfilled life. There is no natural alternative that allows us to prosper. This may sound a bit confusing or backhanded, but it isn't. The Holy Spirit dwells within us, which means God's will literally resides in us physically, in our heart, lungs, and brain. As we are transformed into a new creation with the Holy Spirit, the Holy Spirit has as much place and necessity in our body as any organ does, and if we work against that force in us, it creates unease, conflict, and even severe anxiety. The *only* way is the way ordained for us by God.

*Therefore, if anyone is in Christ, he is a new creation.*
*The old has passed away; behold, the new has come.*
2 Corinthians 5:17, ESV

**Our Calling is Permanent**

*God's gifts and his call are irrevocable.*
Romans 11:29, NIV

I cannot emphasize this enough: the gifts and calling of God are non-negotiable and non-returnable. Our calling is permanent and totally irrevocable. Does this mean if we are called to work in the nursery or the parking lot during church service this week that it's where God will use us throughout our ministry? No; most certainly not. As our spiritual maturity grows, our availability is freed to be used. Our ministry opportunities will blossom.

I have played many roles in my calling, and so will you. This concept is very difficult for most of us to understand. To grasp the permanence of our calling is to fully understand the miracle of God's omnipotence. Once God has called us, He has called us. There is nothing we or anyone around us can do to change His plan. Our spiritual gifts are received at salvation, but our calling is a gift we received at creation. The permanence of this is both confounding and redeeming. It is a beautiful piece of reality when we realize that there is a plan, it is in motion, and we can act as welcome participants in God's works in our life. As I look through the tiny prism of my life, this reality helps me to fully grasp God's love for me and comforts me when I doubt what I see.

What we see is just a sliver of His plan as it unfolds. Hanging in the "Girl Cave" (my old office turned into a TV room for our daughters), is a drawing that Alecia, my eldest, drew many years ago. This artwork is a tapestry of a tree with only the trunk and branches showing. What isn't shown is a larger and more complicated picture underground that is only seen by God. Beneath the surface is a foundational root structure that provides strength, nourishment, and footing. God is also at work in our lives with a labyrinth of planned motion. Alecia captured one of the great Biblical truths in her drawing and revealed the fact that our view is woefully incomplete compared to God's. To be certain, the Lord knows our past, and more importantly, He knows our future. God will never change His mind concerning us, and He will not withdraw whatever spiritual gifts He has given to us. God knows our flaws, our temptations to turn back, and our self-doubt. He created those emotions and certainly accounts for them as He calls us to His will.

Here is the tough part for me: God's will is always done. No matter what obstacle may be in our way in fulfilling His calling, God doesn't redirect around us. He is not looking for a substitute. He is not seeking a *yes* from another. God makes the path clear and doesn't look for alternative plans around us. God routinely steps in to make His will happen. With or without us, His will is done. His will, my will, our will, your will . . . that's a lot of wills. I know this sounds a bit like Lucille Ball telling Ricky Ricardo about her day, but in reality, it just makes sense. Through the Holy Spirit, the God of the universe brings His will to pass.

The permanent and patient will of God was to set aside Israel as His people, even as they were enslaved in Egypt. God sent Moses to stand before Pharaoh and tell him, "Let my people go so they can serve me." It's astonishing how God orchestrates Pharaoh's denials into a grand demonstration of His perfect plan. When Pharaoh refused, God did not hesitate to destroy the land of Egypt, kill their firstborn, and unleash locusts and frogs. There is no king, emperor, or president who can stand against the will of almighty God. Nothing can stand in the way of God Almighty, not even the Red Sea. You can read the full story beginning in Exodus 4.

Nobody can resist the call of God and succeed. God will work with us or in spite of us. Nobody can stop what God has purposed them to do. When the prophet Jonah was sent to warn the people of Nineveh about the impending judgment of God, he did all he could to escape the assignment. God used a raging sea, instilled fear in the sailors, and even ordained a whale to transport him to the shore of the land of Nineveh. Jonah was shocked to discover that the people he thought should perish, repented. From the king down to the animals, they worshiped God. All the land bowed before God.

### Our Calling is Timeless

The ways of God are not our ways, and most of the time, when God is working, we don't fully see or understand what He is doing. Even at times when we think He must be failing, Scripture says He knows the end from the beginning. Even as we will be surrounded by darkness and evil, as prophesied in the book of Revelation, about the future events of Armageddon, we will be in the master plan. I love the Christian saying, "I read the last chapter, and we win!" Certainly, as it relates to the enormity of all past and future, God is a perfect God who can never make a mistake in choosing the person to do His will or by giving out a task at the wrong time. God's timing is always divine. Even when we think he is late or never going to show, His timing is always perfect. I am awed at the sense that even in a very small way, my calling can have the same impact as God's superstars. If the weakest link is truly as important as the strongest, we are all playing a real and significant part in God's master plan.

My testimony to God's timing is, quite frankly, painful. In mid-2014, I was finishing up an aviation business plan that I'd thought about for over twenty years. Yes, twenty years. My ClipperJet plan was the novel that aspiring writers dream about writing but never quite commit the time, energy, and sacrifice needed to get it done. My plan was really more about my dream job and a culmination of my life's work and professional experience. My plan, fortunately, melded well with the current negative airline industry dynamics and market needs that were waiting for a commercial solution. It seemed like the perfect time to pull it all together.

I related to the ClipperJet plan so personally that I could envision every single detail of its creation, operation, and eventual execution. I felt it was what I was made to do. I had built a couple of businesses before, including a very successful aerospace company, but had never jumped off the deep end and taken the risk of leaving the security and steady paycheck of my day job in technology. I risked some savings and much of my spare time but never really put it all out there to be successful. For ClipperJet, God had another idea.

After several months of exploring the possibility and opportunity, my wife and I knew it was something weighing heavily on our hearts. God spoke to us in a real and powerful way. Like any other Sunday, we went to the 11:00 a.m. service at Saddleback Church. As is typical, I had no idea what the sermon was about, but it was one for the ages, focusing on letting go and letting God control everything in our life. Not just a few things or a portion but *everything*. Pastor Rick stuck it right out there, and both Valerie and I realized this plan I'd just finished was, in fact, a calling by God. The Holy Spirit was so convicting that day, we didn't even get to the parking lot before we both realized and agreed we were going to take the leap and follow my calling. That's where the timing insanity begins.

Now, I would love to tell you that in God's divinity and omnipotence, the path was cleared, and everything fell into place like clockwork, but nothing could be farther from the truth. There were many "God Things" along the way, but the journey of pulling ClipperJet together took over three and a half years and cost me virtually all of my personal savings. It brought Valerie and me to tears on many occasions. We were on the brink of losing our faith in a "calling" that had seemed so clear and inspired by God. In our darkest moments, we wondered how so many things could have gone wrong and how a disaster could be looming over us, including near bankruptcy and the potential loss of our home. We were flat broke and deflated. Then, in a burning bush moment, God spoke to us as clearly as possible.

## Whose Job is it Anyway?

Thursday, May 12, 2016, was a day of reckoning for us; it went from the highest high to the lowest low I had ever experienced. Our expectation, from the banker, was that we would finally receive the funding promised after waiting for so long. We could finally purchase our first plane and begin commercial flying operations. The banker expected we would be funded Wednesday, the eleventh.

I, in faith, was interviewing people and preparing the way for our airplane purchase, when I met Bill. Bill is a very experienced aircraft commander and accomplished aviation executive with exactly the skillset, experience, and mindset we needed to round out our management team. In preparation for my interview with Bill, I closely read his resume. I was encouraged to read, in the opening sentence of his cover letter, he had prayerfully considered the opportunity and was excited at its possibilities. I have interviewed and hired many people in my career but have never run across somebody so bold as to say they have "prayerfully considered the opportunity," so I was looking forward to our conversation.

The interview with Bill started in a typical fashion, with him running through his qualifications and management philosophies, which were a great match with ours. The conversation became interesting when we started talking about spiritual things. I told Bill I appreciated his boldness in stating he was prayerful in considering working for us, and we shared our spiritual stories. After hanging up from the interview, I was relieved at the possibility of having Bill join our team and was very excited to have a man of his character lead my flight department. My excitement was quickly transformed into doubt and frustration, yet again.

After hanging up with Bill, I received a call from the banker, who was twenty-four hours late at this point, in funding our bank account. He indicated that, yet again, we had been delayed, and that the funds would not be ours until June 3rd.

To be honest, I lost it with him. I could not understand how we were delayed, again. I could not trust anything he said because nothing he had previously committed to had come true. I am sure you get my frustration. I concluded by telling him I was done, I was out of rope both emotionally and fiscally, and this setback was the straw that broke the camel's back.

I was now in a free fall, realizing the dream of my divinely inspired calling was dead, along with our life savings and all personal resources. I was now a letdown to ClipperJet investors and my family, who supported me along the way. Valerie and I spent several hours that evening lamenting, questioning, and crying about what was left for us. We felt not just the financial loss, but in essence, the loss of our witness to the many friends, small group, family, and colleagues who knew that ClipperJet was more than a business proposition. It was our "calling," and we had placed our faith in God and His word that He would see us through. The reality of that day was He had not, and the pain of that reality was like receiving a blow to the head. I told Valerie I felt like Noah, praying for rain that was so clearly promised yet never came.

However, in the midst of one of the darkest days, God revealed Himself in an unmistakable way. He used a willing servant in Bill to speak to us. Bill sent this email that night, while Valerie and I were feeling as alone and upended as two people possibly could:

*"Mr. Occhipinti,*
*Greetings from New Orleans!!!*
*So . . . while I was wandering around Bourbon Street tonight, you [specifically] kept coming to mind (OK . . . to be completely transparent . . . you . . . specifically . . . were not the ONLY thing that kept coming to mind during my wanderings . . .), and I do not know . . . if . . . at this present time your bank account has had a "population explosion"*

*recently, however . . . what did keep coming to mind were the words . . .For I know the plans and thoughts that I have for you, James Occhipinti,' says the Lord, 'plans for peace and well-being and not for disaster . . . to give you a future and a hope. Then you will call on Me and you will come and pray to Me, and I will hear your voice and I will listen to you . . . Then with a deep longing you will seek Me and require Me as a vital necessity and you will find Me when you search for Me with all your heart. I WILL BE FOUND BY YOU,' says the Lord, 'and I will restore your fortunes and I will FREE YOU and gather you from all the nations and from all the places where I have driven you,' says the Lord, 'and I will bring you back to the place from where I sent you into exile. Jeremiah 29, KJV*

*Sorry . . . I am kinda an Amplified Bible guy . . . please understand that this is difficult for me . . . and NOT the usual email interaction for me . . .*

*Look . . . I do not know if these words presented in this email are a benefit to you . . . OR . . . if they are some kind of 'slam in the face to your faith,' however . . . this night and at this present time in your life . . . these words have truly been on my mind FOR YOU JAMES . . . SPECIFICALLY . . .*

*I imagine these days have been very hard for you, and your family . . . and . . . your business team . . . HOWEVER . . . all I can add is, "But first and most importantly seek (aim at, strive after) His kingdom and His righteousness [His way of doing and being right—the attitude and character of God], and ALL these things will be given to you also" (Mathew 6:33-34 AMP).*

*Sorry, I could not sleep unless I presented to you these words tonight . . . Respectfully, and my best wishes, Bill*

I do not believe in coincidence, and I certainly do not believe this message was random inspiration from a person I had never met and had only talked to once. For Valerie and me, it was a burning bush, and it was God telling us He loved us, He heard us, and He had not forgotten us. It was a reminder we needed to have just a little more faith and endurance-—to hold on a little longer. Though it is commonly believed God never gives us more than we can handle, I am here to tell you, in our case, He brought us right to the brink before He was ready to make the path straight.

Our callings are serious business to God. "To whom much is given much is expected" (Luke 12:48, NIV), and the testing in that process is sometimes astonishingly painful. During the time of waiting on God, I can't tell you the amount of things that went wrong. You probably wouldn't believe me if I did, but the following is true: God had it. Although it is really difficult for me to say, we must rejoice in the process because, though the refiner's fire is horribly hot, we are purified, sanctified, and made more pleasing to God in the process.

**False Advertisement**

I have often thought, "Are we really telling the truth when we evangelize in the name of Jesus?" We speak of glory, as we set a vision for salvation but never talk about the valleys sure to come. The truth is, every believer will be put through the refiner's fire. I am not alone in my personal journey through the valleys of fear, confusion, and dismay. Every believer will have to endure a trip through a valley, and some of us will get many painful journeys.

Scripture is very, very clear that God is the God of the

valley. Pastor Rick has often preached God is the Master of all, not just the good.

*God is our refuge and strength,*
*an ever-present help in trouble.*
*Therefore we will not fear, though the earth*
*give way and the mountains fall into the heart*
*of the sea, though its waters roar and foam*
*and the mountains quake with their surging.*

*There is a river whose streams make glad the city*
*of God, the holy place where the Most High*
*dwells. God is within her, she will not fall;*
*God will help her at break of day.*
*Nations are in uproar, kingdoms fall;*
*he lifts his voice, the earth melts.*

*The Lord Almighty is with us;*
*the God of Jacob is our fortress.*

*Come and see what the Lord has done,*
*the desolations he has brought on the earth.*
*He makes wars cease to the ends of the earth.*
*He breaks the bow and shatters the spear;*
*he burns the shields[d] with fire.*
*He says, "Be still, and know that I am God;*
*I will be exalted among the nations,*
*I will be exalted in the earth."*

*The Lord Almighty is with us;*
*the God of Jacob is our fortress.*
Psalm 46, NIV

I do not believe God's will is bad for us, but I am convinced God uses the bad to develop us in Jesus' image. To become Christ-like means a trip or two through our Gardens of Gethsemane.

As I look back on my life, I could never have predicted the series of walks through the valley I would take throughout the years, and the truth is that as we age, and our experiences expand, we are guaranteed to endure more. It is impossible to predict the tragedies of our lives and the frequency and magnitude of them, but I know, now more than ever, that I am not alone. I walk with the creator of the universe, and in those times I think I am alone, I am assured the footprints behind me are His as He carries me through.

I took great solace and hope in the writings of Pastor Lon Solomon, of the McLean Bible Church, in Virginia. In his book, *Brokenness*, Solomon describes his most painful journey and how God made His presence known in the process. Sharing his darkest days, Solomon's writing relays how God uses the refiner's fire to mold us into Christ's image and how, in the process, we become more like Him. We can't become Christ-like in our faith without enduring a fraction of the pain endured by Jesus on the Via Dolorosa, Jesus' painful and bloody path to the cross. If you ever find yourself in the refiner's fire, get Solomon's book. The Lord will powerfully speak to you.

## Calling Means Connection

*There is one body and one Spirit, just as you were called to one hope when you were called . . .*
Ephesians 4:4, NIV

Nobody is called to fulfill the work of God alone. There is no Superman in the fold of God. Each of us is called to do only a part of the job, which is complemented by the efforts of others who are equally called to do their work with us. In the great tapestry of God's work, there is a connection between my missionary work in Africa and Mother Teresa's missionary work in Calcutta. There is a connection between my church planting efforts as a college student at the Cherry Creek Wesleyan Church in Colorado, and the great Mission building in California, by the Catholic Church, or even my feeble writings on these pages and the great writings of C.S. Lewis, as he took us on his inspired journeys. Somehow, in His grand and elaborate plan, God places His people in the play of His creation. Some of us play small or seemingly incomplete parts, and some have leading roles, but all are integral to His will. The Apostle Paul said, "As it is, there are many parts, but one body" (1 Corinthians 12:20, KJV). That is true in all situations. For all ministries and ministers, our work is never complete. It is simply carried on. It is our role to operate within the limitations of the work God has given us today, and others will have to come in to do their own part as His will unfolds.

We are all one body in Christ, but we all have different roles. Just like the parts of our physical bodies, each person is playing a role to make the body of Christ function as it ought to.

This is the reason there are pastors, priests, evangelists, prophets, and teachers in the kingdom. This is also why there are Sunday school teachers, workers at the church food bank, and coaches for the church softball team. It is why God refuses to give all the responsibility to one person or group. I firmly believe God is indifferent to whether you receive your paycheck from the church or from somewhere else. We are all called, we are all ministers, and we are all ordained with His call on our life.

*I have planted, Apollos watered; but God gave the increase.*
1 Corinthians 3:6, KJV

The question is, how is it that people from different backgrounds, cultures, educational statuses, and experiences are able to work together and have the same goals, mission, and drive, as is the case within the Christian Church? The church is at one with different doctrines here on earth, even though we may bear different denominational names. As far as God, the owner of the church, is concerned, the Church is one, and it will always remain so. Rick Warren has often said, the only constant throughout the expanse of time—past, present, and future—is the church. No government, no currency, no company, and no building has or will stand the test of time. Only the church has and will continue to. As history shows us, man's creation is flawed and susceptible to destruction. Only God's creation and the church will last into eternity.

Even with the denominational and doctrinal divisions, what we see today is the manifestation of the Holy Spirit at work in the world. The Spirit of God in the Church is the power that has kept the church alive, and through all of the persecutions and evil works recorded against the church throughout the history of man, the church survives and thrives. Even man's flaws in the church are not enough to bring it down. Just yesterday, we had a guest pastor, from Saddleback Church Hong Kong, report that in just a few short months, since starting, they have grown from a few to over 400 saved lives.

The Spirit of God has the power to fuse together every individual who belongs to the kingdom of God. Even a culturally primitive pygmy from the thick forest of the Congo in Africa can relate to and bond with an aristocrat from England. An NFL quarterback from the U.S. and a ping pong player from China, a prima ballerina from Russia, and a break dancer from the streets of New York—when people of all types are fused with the Holy Spirit, the attraction is inevitable. I have witnessed this many times and have said to my wife or daughters, "I just sense the Spirit in that person." Recently, I was reminded of this while watching my favorite pastime, Formula One Racing.

Nineteen times per year, I set my DVR to record races from all over the world—from the cobblestone streets of Monaco in Europe to the perfectly engineered track in Singapore—I watch with amazement as young drivers from around the world pilot their automotive wonders at speeds unfathomable for most mortals. F1 is truly amazing, and perhaps the most amazing driver, at least this year, is a young British driver named Lewis Hamilton. Now, in all honesty, I am not a very good fan of most sports, even F1. I love sports and admittedly watch F1, football, and most any in-season sport, but I'm really not a dedicated fan. I don't read about what is going on in the lives of the teams, the players, or even the drivers. I don't pay attention to statistics and rarely am I the first to know about a big trade or a big deal contract. I simply watch week after week, formulating my favorite teams and drivers based on their performance on the field or on the track.

Here is where it gets interesting. Since his debut in Formula 1, in 2007, I have been drawn to team Mercedes' driver Lewis Hamilton, not just because he wins races—and he has won more than his share—or because he has driven for two of the great historic F1 teams, Williams and Mercedes Benz, or because I have parked a Mercedes Benz in my garage over the years, but because I was truly drawn to his spirit. It all made sense to me when, during the last race of the 2017 season, the British Grand Prix of which Hamilton was the winner, it was mentioned in passing, by the race commentator, that Hamilton is a devout Christian and very true to his Catholic faith.

In a bold and daring move, Hamilton has now removed all questions, by placing a tattoo on the left side of his neck, just above his collar line, that reads, "GOD is Good." I am convinced that when two Spirit-filled people come together, even when they are thousands of miles apart and brought together through satellites and modern television technology, they see the same spirit in each other because the same Holy Spirit is working in them. It is my desire to have all see the Holy Spirit living in me. This is one of the great secrets of God that is operating in the church, one which the world cannot comprehend.

Through the Holy Spirit, we are all connected, as God lives in us. God reveals our gifts, purpose, and ordained responsibility shared among God's people for the edification of the church. Our calling is designed by God for the building and growth of all the members so the will and purposes of God are accomplished. It is that spirit that also links all individual gifts in the church together and channels them towards the same common goal of proclaiming the authority and Lordship of Christ, establishing His Kingdom here on earth.

It is the same Holy Spirit that engages everyone in the Church to be useful for God. It does not matter how we started our lives, or what state we were in when we confessed our desire to serve God—the Holy Spirit directs us to where we belong in the fold and makes us flourish in the office God has ordained for us, all for His glory.

When the Holy Spirit is given the opportunity to do His will in the Church, only heaven can predict what will happen. The actions and powers of the Apostles, illustrated in the Bible, are actually the acts of the Holy Spirit in the lives of the Apostles. Through the Holy Spirit, a fearful Peter preached earth-shaking sermons bringing thousands to God. The Holy Spirit made Philip confident in his preaching, as he delivered joyful messages to the entire city. The Holy Spirit caused an earthquake to tear down the walls of a prison and liberate His people from the captivity of the enemy. The Holy Spirit is the power of God in the Church. I can't help but call out all we are missing in the church because we have become lazy or apathetic toward the Holy Spirit. In most churches, and certainly most denominations, the power of the Holy Spirit has become somewhat of a mystery or ambiguity. We have never really fully realized the power of the Holy Spirit or why we, in the church, tend to look to the power of Jesus and God the Father, but rely less on the Holy Spirit, even though our faith declares the Holy Spirit as an equal part in the Trinity.

## EIGHT

# God Empowers Our Calling

*The One who calls you is faithful and he will do it.*
1 Thessalonians 5:24, NIV

God does not just call us and leave us to do the work all alone. Whatever God calls us to, He will equip us properly to ensure nothing will stand in our way of accomplishing success for Him. In fact, when we feel the *least* capable is when we lean on Him for strength, understanding, and direction. Trust me; writing this book is a perfect example. It takes the power of God to do the work of God. We stumble when we get in the way. Things get messy or off-kilter when we let our pride or our own will infuse God's plan. Scripture says, "By strength shall no man prevail" (1 Samuel 2:9, KJV).

*With this in mind, we constantly pray for you, that our God may make you worthy of his calling, and that by his power he may bring to fruition your every desire for goodness and your every deed prompted by faith.*
2 Thessalonians 1:11, NIV

God is the only one who can make us worthy of His calling because He knows the enormity of what lies ahead of us. After the resurrection of Jesus, He told the disciples, before He ascended to Heaven, they would be visited by the Holy Spirit and would receive power from the Holy Ghost, who would come upon them as witnessed in Jerusalem, Judea, and all over the world. Today, their witness continues in the long line of work that is never finished; work which continues into eternity.

At the time Jesus spoke of the Holy Spirit's coming, there was no real indication of the work ahead. The disciples and followers of Jesus felt despair about His pending death; they saw their hopes and dreams dashed, and they saw a huge injustice at the hands of Herods's strike, as they all had left everything to follow Jesus. Through the Trinity, the Holy Spirit picked up at the cross and is present everywhere God is at work. Had Jesus been a mere man, the chapter would be over, just one more cult leader meeting his demise. But through the Holy Spirit, God's work lives on, and Jesus lives in us daily. God's ordination of the Holy Spirit changed everything and nothing all at once. Through the work of the Holy Spirit, Jesus has been vindicated as God's perfect plan, and the escalation of God's work only intensifies through every action in the chain.

On the day of Pentecost, the Holy Spirit came and filled the church with a new power. From that day forward, the followers of Jesus ceased to be terrified by any man—any enemy of God; their world was turned upside down for God.

That same power of the Holy Spirit is still real and at work today; it did not die with the Apostles. Jesus Christ is the same yesterday, today, and forever. He has not changed even a little bit. He still equips and prepares for God's work, even as He is calling people into His vineyard today. Who is the next rock star for God? Looking back at Christian powerhouses, we have seen many people emerge from obscurity to wonder in the name of God. I continue to be amazed at who God has chosen.

*Then saith he unto his disciples, The harvest truly is plenteous, but the laborers are few; Pray ye therefore the*

# God Empowers Our Calling

*Lord of the harvest, that he will send forth laborers into his harvest.*
Matthew 9:37-38, KJV

There is an undeniable call for everyone to wake up, take their place in the Kingdom of God, and act on their callings. The earnest expectation of the creation is waiting for the manifestation of the sons of God. When we accept His call, receive His power, and serve Him diligently, only then will the will of God be done on earth as it is in Heaven.

NINE

# Our Calling is God's Love

The defining factor that characterizes our relationship with God is love. Love inspired God to create us in His image, love is why God did not destroy us when Adam fell in the Garden of Eden, and God's complete love for us inspired Him to place Jesus in the world to die for us and rescue us from the bondage of sin. It is for love, and only because of love, that we exist.

*For God so loved the world that he gave his one and only Son, that whoever believes in him shall not perish but have eternal life.*
John 3:16, NIV

The love God has for us is so strong, human words and experiences do not adequately explain it, and that is why the Bible instructs us to understand that God is love (John 4:8). The love of God is so strong, nothing in existence can stop it, meaning, nothing can make God stop loving us. What wonderful news!

*No, in all these things we are more than conquerors through him who loved us. For I am convinced that neither death nor life, neither angels nor demons, neither the present nor the future, nor any powers, neither height nor depth, nor anything else in all creation, will be able to separate us*

*from the love of God that is in Christ Jesus our Lord.*
Romans 8:37-39, NIV

This is the reason it is so easy for God to reach out to the worst sinner—love compels God. God is obsessed with us, and He thinks about us continually. His obsession over us also covers our areas of calling. Out of love, God can call a sinner in His sinful state, wash him of any dirt or filth, and then fully equip him for the assignments He ordained for him.

Can you imagine how painful it is for God when we spurn His love and reject His calling? It happened with man in the Garden of Eden. God made him the apex of His creation, put all things under his feet, and gave him dominion over all he created, yet man chose to follow Satan rather than God by eating the forbidden fruit. Still, God did not completely reject man, even though He drove him away from the garden. He allowed man to live, and He provided comfort for him.

The love God has for us allows Him to choose the type of life He wants us to live, and it is the highest and best form of life, which is why man is so distinct from other creatures. We are special in God's eyes.

Only God's love can facilitate the life we were meant to live. Where there is an atmosphere of God's love, everything He created will work together for the good of man and will minister to His needs. Embedded in God's love is the totality of all He wants us to have.

### God Wants His Love in US

*And hope does not disappoint us, because God has poured out his love into our hearts by the Holy Spirit, whom he has given us. You see, at just the right time, when we were still powerless, Christ died for the ungodly. Very rarely will anyone die for a righteous man, though for*

*a good man someone might possibly dare to die. But God demonstrates his own love for us in this: While we were still sinners, Christ died for us.*
Romans 5:5-8, NIV

This is a very crucial revelation given to the Apostle Paul. God does not only want His Spirit living in us; He also wants His love to manifest *through* us. He wants us to love just like Him. The implication of this is that we will be able to love like God, or better said, God through the Holy Spirit will love through us. God made us in His own image. His image is love—God is love and He loves all, even the unlovable, the thief on the cross next to Jesus, Bernie Madoff, Charles Manson, and countless others who society has deemed as unlovable. Through Jesus, God shows love to these people, despite the fact that they lived the kind of life most would not wish to identify with. They can be termed as the enemies of God, yet He loved them to the point of saving them from their plight. He loved them in a way which can only be defined as divine.

This type of love is not common among men, and as a matter of fact, it is hardly ever seen outside of the church and Christian institutions. What secular man calls love is loving those who love them back and hating those who hate them. In secular terms, we feel justified that hating those who hate us is okay, but through the power of the Holy Spirit, we are compelled to love through God's power and not our own. As Americans, we could not be more divided. We must resist that which divides us and embrace the love of God, which binds us and liberates us through the Spirit. This is not to say we are not sometimes challenged by this.

I had a situation happen recently which has forced me to really try to come to terms with my secular or carnal nature. I typically live my life in a very positive manner and am very aware of the grace bestowed on me, and I try to grant grace to others. It was a day like any other, and in a split second, I was forced into what could have been a life-or-death situation. I will only say that carnal James emerged, and he can be pretty ugly.

After visiting my daughter Tori at Pepperdine University recently, I stopped for gas. Malibu is a very small coastal town on the Pacific Coast Highway just north of Los Angeles. It is known as a quiet and sleepy oasis for the Hollywood elite and home to the who's who in the entertainment industry, but for me, it became a potential life-or-death nightmare. While getting gas, I was confronted by a kid between eighteen and twenty years old, asking for money. I politely replied, "I don't have any money," which was the truth. My wallet was empty. I'd just paid cash for dinner, and I was completely out. Upon hearing my response, this individual became aggressive and moved closer to me, while reaching for something in his pocket.

Quite frankly, I snapped. I felt the blood rush to my head, my heart started beating a million miles per second, and I went into survival mode. The only thing I could think to do was grab the fuel nozzle out of the car and point it straight at him, and in my darkest, deepest voice, I told him to stop: "Don't even think about it, or you will get a shower of gasoline, and then I will crush your head into that gas pump." I told him I was 250 pounds (a bit of an exaggeration), and he was 125, so it wouldn't end well for him. And by the grace of God, and perhaps the presence of a couple of angels, he stopped and just stared at me.

Fortunately, someone else came up—I think someone he knew—and I used the distraction to make an escape. Did the kid have a knife or a gun? I don't know because I never saw it, but I will tell you the carnal James was prepared to kill if I had to, and that scared the "you know what" out of me. As I continue to relive those few moments, I ask myself, "Was my response that of a man living with God's love in him, or was my response a reflex of carnality?" I don't know. What I do know is, I praise God I made it out of that situation without being harmed or harming that kid, even with his ill intent for me.

I do know that as Jesus was faced with death at the hand of Pontius Pilate, His reaction was a bit different than mine. I have thought, on occasion, that I missed an opportunity with this kid. Who knows what he was up against: hunger, homelessness? . . . Could I have used the moment to witness, reach out, and show the love of Christ? I don't know. Fear is a very powerful emotion.

*But Jesus was saying, "Father, forgive them;*
*for they do not know what they are doing."*
Luke 23:34a, NASB

This is the highest form of love possible; there, on the cross, was the Savior of the world who came to save mankind—who lived in hunger, suffering, and all kinds of deprivation for us. Man punished Him down the Via Dolorosa and hung Him on a cross at Golgotha, even though He did them no wrong and never did any wrong throughout His sinless life.

According to carnal impulse and secular reasoning, Jesus ought to curse His accusers as He did the fruitless fig tree, but He prayed for them because He loved them despite what they did to Him. He could have called down fire upon them like in the days of Elijah. He could even have asked His Father for angelic reinforcement to quickly destroy all His captors and prove to them that He was the Almighty, but He never did that. Like a sheep before the slaughter, He surrendered to all their humiliations and punishment and died a shameful death. Only God can love like that.

Hatred is often misguided or ignorant. Growing up

Italian and Roman Catholic, I knew many people with what can only be described as a hatred for Jews. I can't say that I, or anybody I know, knew a Jew at that time, but because of what "they" did to Jesus, it was okay to hate them. To hate the Jews, because of their ancestors' hand in the execution of Jesus is to completely miss the sacrifice and lesson of Jesus' forgiveness and salvation. It is to completely miss God's plan for man. Also, is it not ironic that, though Jesus was executed at the insistence of the Jews, it was actually by the hand of the Romans the execution was carried out?

Preaching the gospel is a task God committed to our hands; we are to seek the lost, wherever they are, in any part of the world, and preach the gospel of the kingdom to them, so they can be saved and see the love God has for them. What this translates to is we need to deny ourselves of our time, resources, and even freedom sometimes. For this to be possible, we need God's kind of love.

The world, with its own understanding, is not ready to accept the gospel of Christ. Many are hostile to the name of Jesus Christ, but the commission still remains, and the world must be reached. What can make a man leave his family, country, or homeland to go to strange places to preach the gospel without hoping to get any monetary reward or human commendation, if there is no love driving the action?

When Jesus walked on earth, He loved sinners. He ate with them, related to them, and kept their company, to the point that the Pharisees complained He was a sinner along with them. Divine love caused Jesus to go to all men and reach them as God incarnate. He knew that man would see God and realize their need and desire for Him through the love He showed them.

God does not see man as sinners condemned to Hell. He sees us as the objects of His affection, in the same way a parent sees a child. As Christians, we must see all men through the same prism. We must not condemn them but grieve in our hearts for them if they are on a path away from His love. This is our inspiration—our calling—as we seek to introduce people all around us to the gift of love we have. This desire is why we are Sunday school teachers, ushers, missionaries, and small group hosts. We invite people into our homes to share a love only available through God. For me, sharing God's love is the most important job.

God's love for us helps us to love Him. This sounds a bit confusing. It is difficult to love a God you do not see and that you cannot relate with physically, but when His love dwells in our hearts, we will be able to reach out to Him and love Him as He is. Love is God. He is defined by it, and frankly, His physical touch on us is His love for us.

God's first commandment is to "Love the Lord your God with all your heart, with all your soul, with all your strength, and with all your mind" (Luke 10:27, NIV). How can we, as selfish and self-centered people, love like that, except through He who plants His divine love in our hearts? We will seek to do things that please and avoid hurting Him, just as we find it difficult to hurt the feelings of someone we love dearly. This is the best and surest way of doing the will of God—find the way of love, and we find God.

As God, Jesus looks to be assured of Peter's love after His resurrection in John 21:

*When they had finished eating, Jesus said to Simon Peter,*
*"Simon son of John, do you love me more than these?"*
*"Yes, Lord," he said, "you know that I love you."*
*Jesus said, "Feed my lambs." Again Jesus said,*
*"Simon son of John, do you love me?" He answered,*
*"Yes, Lord, you know that I love you."*
*Jesus said, "Take care of my sheep."*
*The third time he said to him, "Simon son of John,*

*do you love me?" Peter was hurt because Jesus asked him the third time, "Do you love me?" He said, "Lord, you know all things; you know that I love you." Jesus said, "Feed my sheep.*
John 21:15-17, ASV

Why did Jesus pester Peter so much by asking over and over if Peter loved Him? Was Peter lacking intelligence? I don't think so. Was Peter demonstrating disobedience or disillusionment? I don't think this is the case either. Jesus is persistent because He knows that only genuine love for Him can see Peter through–keep him devoted to his calling and purpose later in his ministry.

We all know Peter loved Jesus. He actually wanted to die with Him, but he soon realized he could only do this as far as his physical strength could carry him, because by strength, shall no man prevail. He denied the one he loved even in the presence of a little girl, but when the love of God became strong upon him after he received the Holy Ghost, he was able to love more and do more through God's love, even in the face of death.

There really is something to this. When God was present, either through Jesus in the flesh or through the Holy Spirit, Peter was empowered equally. The love of God makes our world a better place. All the evils being perpetrated today come as a result of a lack of love. The Bible says to love your neighbor as you love yourself, meaning that whatever you wish for yourself is what you should wish for your neighbor. That cannot be possible for a natural man, but with the love of God in us, we can do it.

Jesus demonstrated this to us in this way: He was the sole heir to the Kingdom of His Father, but He wanted many joint heirs to inherit the kingdom with Him, hence He went out to seek and save those who were lost and bring them into the kingdom. When the hold that Satan had over God's people was too strong, He offered to die in their place to save them from the clutch of Sin. Evil is real. Some of the best minds'-eye illustrations in modern times came through the writings and imaginations of C.S. Lewis and J.R.R. Tolkien, who both demonstrate evil for what it really is. They find the evils within us as strong and compelling as the tyrannical evils imposed on man by others, who are usually in a quest for power or acting out of selfish desire. Never is evil exposed to us as the bogey-man or a deep red creature with horns. We fight evil daily in the forms of selfishness, vanity, and personal desire.

God's divine love is the highest form of love demonstrated by Jesus, because He did not die for only the good people, the perfect people, or the Priests and Rabbis of the day, but for all of us, even the "bad", who do not reserve any place in their hearts for Him. It is when we are carrying a Jesus-like love that we can actually love like Him.

When we love our neighbors, we will not wish them evil or do any harm against them. We will protect their interest and seek for their well-being at all times. We will not covet their properties or get envious of their attainments. All of these are manifestations of the human flesh, and they pale into insignificance and generally fade out when the love of God takes over.

Our love for God helps us obey Him. Obeying God is sacrificial. All of the things that He asks us are not what our flesh wants and can sometimes result in pain and discomfort when we obey Him. God's love is stronger than fear, hence we find it easier to obey out of love rather than out of fear.

When we love, we find it easy to give anything. The Bible recorded that Solomon loved the Lord, and as a result of that, he sacrificed a thousand offerings, and God blessed him with the gift of wisdom. The love Solomon had for God made him see past the value of the sacrifice he committed, and instead, he desired to fill the void in him. So, Solomon kept sacrificing until his void vanished. This sacrifice cannot fully be understood until we realize the sacrifice of Jesus on the cross. It was God's love for us which drove Him to such a meaningful sacrifice on Calvary.

It is the love God has for us that makes Him hear us when we cry to Him in prayer, not because we deserve answers or blessings from Him, but because He loves us. He will hear us and answer our requests, albeit sometimes in the form of "no" or "wait." The love is so strong that if a chronic sinner comes to God for forgiveness and for a new life, God will answer immediately with no conditions, no secret handshakes, no hazing, and no proof of worthiness. It's immediate, and it's forever. I am struck by what this instant and unconditional readmission means. God, throughout the ages, plucks the most unworthy and gives them an assignment. A few things always accompany us in the process—God always meets us where we are, God always calms our fears, and most importantly, God always shows us His power and that He will use it through us as we honor and obey Him. For me, it is easy to accept my calling when I know it is through His power, not mine.

In his book *Ex-Muslim*, Naeem Fazal demonstrates his supernatural calling and God's power in his life when he was drawn to Jesus. He was forced to risk the rejection of his family, friends, and even death, as he denounced Islam and believed instead in God's revelation through Jesus Christ.[6]

Fazal's story is also the story of every man and woman who comes to Christ. Granted, most are not risking death, and each person's story will be told in different forms and with different details. You have to leave or forsake something in order to gain Christ, and often, we will face persecution and rejection. One thing that will help you carry on, despite all of this, is the love of God—the love that made Him die for us regardless of who we were.

## Our Calling is God's Love

To most Americans, the notion of religious persecution has, until recently, only been something we read about, but not something any of us have really ever had to deal with. Christian persecution has been the norm throughout the ages, but our generation has been insulated from its horrors until now. All over the news today are images of Christians being herded onto mountain tops to starve or be beheaded because of their refusal to accept Islam. Clearly, times are changing. Faith has become the pariah of the entertainment industry, the Higher Education elites, and most recently, by the news media who now routinely paint traditional Christianity as bigotry and intolerance.

There is no doubt that through the loveless acts of some Christians, all of us get painted in a bad light. But I like to remind our critics that the actions of a very few should not detract from the great work by the millions who work for good in God's kingdom. I ask the naysayers to pay attention when they drive the streets of their towns and see the many churches scattered about. Each one of those buildings represents hundreds, if not thousands, of people who congregate each week for good and for God.

We are all born into a belief system and a particular religion or the belief that there is no God. God knew how we would be raised before we were a twinkle in our parents' eyes. We were His before we were theirs. He knew what religion our parents were before, bringing us into the world through them. He knows the challenges we will face and what pushback we will get, but He also knows that with His calling comes His power. God, through Jesus, will reveal His love and His calling on us in His time. For some of us, the call comes when we are young, but for many, it comes late. God's light shines the brightest in our darkest moments. I believe one of the reasons why He allows dark moments in our lives is so we may have a taste of what life outside Christ is like, so we clearly understand what His love really means.

By now, you might be asking yourself, "Why is he going on and on about love? This is a book about my calling and how important it is. Why all the 'God loves me' stuff?" Let me answer by saying two things. First, love is absolutely and without question the reason for your calling, and without understanding that God's love drives everything, then our callings are meaningless. Second, there is way too little love in the world! People are divided. Today, disagreement has been translated into hate. Secularly, hate is winning, but love must prevail.

"Baltimore is burning" today, because there is an absence of love in that community. Again, the next few thoughts are not in any way meant to be political. They are, instead, meant to demonstrate that where there is an absence of God's love, nothing makes sense, but when God reveals His love through us, everything makes sense. The Baltimore riots in 2015, as well as those re-sparked in 2021, were because of racially motivated prejudice and injustice in our legal and political system–systematic race division. The people of Baltimore hit the streets in protest, burning and looting their own neighborhoods because they felt the injustice and prejudice in the system. Why? There is a complete and utter breakdown of love in our culture. *Phileo* love, "brotherly love," is now almost completely absent.

Two voices in the wilderness have shouted to a great audience lately, and perhaps people are starting to listen. On his personal Facebook on November 26, 2014, Benjamin Watson, an African American NFL tight end with the New Orleans Saints posted the following:

"I'M ANGRY because the stories of injustice that have been passed down for generations seem to be continuing before our very eyes," he began.

But Watson did not stop there. He went on to highlight some very real truths about race and racism in America before noting: "I'M SYMPATHETIC, because I wasn't there so I don't know exactly what happened. Maybe Darren Wilson acted within his rights and duty as an officer of the law and killed Michael Brown in self-defense like any of us would in the circumstance. Now he has to fear the backlash against himself and his loved ones when he was only doing his job. What a horrible thing to endure. OR maybe he provoked Michael and ignited the series of events that led to him eventually murdering the young man to prove a point."[7]

This post received over a million views at the last count, but the real story was what Watson said when he was interviewed by all of the network news channels: CNN, Fox News, MSNBC, etc. In his opinion, the reason for all of the violence and reaction is simple: love is absent in our culture, specifically, the saving love of Jesus Christ. Watson could not be more correct, and his voice is being heard.

Another voice of reason is a dear friend of mine, Dr. Everett Piper, President of Oklahoma Wesleyan University. While being interviewed on a major news channel on the subject of religion being under attack in America today, Dr. Piper said, "Our social conversation is confusing and intended to divide." Dr. Piper revealed the real basis of the conversation, "I cannot tolerate your intolerance and I hate you, hateful people." Our social divide is so great today that cultural disagreement has turned into hating our neighbor.

In the absence of love, the reason is unrecognizable, and the sheer volume of conflict creates confusion. Think about this: culturally, we have replaced love with tolerance. Piper asked, "On Valentine's Day, did you give your wife a card that said 'I really tolerate you'? No, and there is a good reason—to say I tolerate you is an insult. To tolerate someone is to say, 'I don't care who you are, what you do, or what you believe.' We have replaced love in our culture with tolerance, and the law of unintended consequences roars its ugly head. The Christian community must elevate this conversation and redefine cultural expectations to Christian love, a love displayed through our callings. Love says we care more deeply than tolerance. Love says we care deeply rather than I care nothing at all."[8] He is spot on.

*For you were called to freedom, brothers. Only do not use your freedom as an opportunity for the flesh, but through love serve one another.*
Galatians 5:13, ESV

The good news is, that just when you think all of hell is breaking loose and our culture is too far gone, God steps in and says, "Look at what happens when my love prevails!" He turns a horrific situation, perpetrated by a madman, into an almost unbelievable act of love and forgiveness. On June 17th, 2015, the Emanuel African Methodist Episcopal Church in downtown Charleston, South Carolina, came under fire by a crazed and hate-filled young man by the name of Dylann Roof. The event culminated in the death of eight worshippers and the senior Pastor. Roof attacked, in a flurry of gunfire, with the sole purpose of starting a race war.

Virtually every American watched and waited for the protests to begin, poised for the worst of humanity to roar its ugly head, but God had another idea. Less than twenty-four hours after the horrible attacks, and before any of the deceased could be laid to rest, an amazing act of God's love was displayed for the world to see. Instead of hate and rage, all of the families of the victims came out publicly and extended forgiveness to Roof. They prayed for him and witnessed to him, demonstrating his soul was more important than his crime against them. Being obedient to Christ's message and His extinction of forgiveness meant they must forgive.

## Our Calling is God's Love

What an example they were to all of us—to the world. Every one of us should aspire to such spiritual maturity. This display of God's love was so swift and so unexpected, it caught everyone off guard. The media questioned it, with a complete lack of understanding; the politicians stumbled with exactly where to go with it, but God's people knew exactly what to do. They came forward in solidarity and marched the streets of Charleston in love. As I looked through the crowds of thousands, I saw every ethnicity unified under the message of love. God's love wins!

*"He will not shout or cry out, or raise*
*his voice in the streets."*
Isaiah 42:2, NIV

The restoration of love in our society is critical, and the Charleston example must become the norm.

Al Franken is screaming "liar", while Ann Coulter is yelling "treason!" Shock factor is everywhere in our society—it sells books, it stimulates news ratings, it sells advertising, and it commands an audience. Incivility has filtered into the leadership of the church, and worse, into the witness of the church. Our responsibility is simple: represent Christ's love, saving grace, and the gift of salvation to our neighbors, and assist where and when we can. I must admit, it took me forty-five years to realize that civility is an art, not a science. My wife accuses me of not arguing or "fighting fair." She points out that I rarely take my "opponent's" feelings into account when trying to prove my point, because as we all know, "I am always right." I take it personally, I make it personal, and I drive it home with the facts.

Now, in my defense, I was raised in a typical, crazy Italian family where arguing was more the norm than the exception. A family of seven, we routinely fought, argued, and bantered. Skill in the art of arguing was a rite of passage to us—it was claiming your place at the table, it was a process of the natural order, it was eat or be eaten.

Many years ago, my sister brought home a boyfriend for Thanksgiving dinner. Jim was new to the fold, had not spent much time with any of us yet, and certainly had not experienced us as a "group." A couple of hours into the celebration, I noticed Jim alone in the front yard. I decided to check in on him, as I realized we can be a bit overwhelming. Jim was looking a little perplexed, so I asked what he thought of the family, knowing that was his source of tension. Jim's response was classic: he furrowed his brow and deliberately paused to make sure he articulated his statement in a non-confrontational way. After what was more than an uncomfortable amount of awkward silence, he stated simply, "I have never seen so many people arguing and yelling at each other without anybody being mad at anybody." I laughed and said, "You don't know much about Italian families, do you?" He simply shrugged his shoulders and lit a cigarette. He didn't last—he and my sister broke up not long after. Hmm . . . I wonder?!

Incivility in our culture can't infiltrate the church without catastrophic consequences. Here's what I mean: Will God bless the witness of pride and arrogance? Will He bless our opinion and not His? Is insensitivity one of the fruits of the spirit? Will God bless a sermon designed to make a political statement and not a spiritual statement that is based on His love and His word? Our responsibility, as the Church, as Christians, is to be uniters, not dividers. It is to be His ambassador in a foreign land. It is to carry His water, not ours. We must rid ourselves of pride and arrogance before we can truly represent God. Then, and only then, will God truly use us in a big way. Then, and only then, can God trust us.

In defense of myself and others, whose emotions sometimes run a-muck, God knows our hearts, and He knows our intent. In the end, He will allow even our self-centered moments to work for His glory. But, man, can we look less than brilliant in the process?

When Jesus instructed the disciples, knowing they would suffer unreceptive crowds, He simply said, "Shake the dust off your feet," and just move on (Mathew 10:14, ESV). They were to deliver His message and leave the rest to man's free will and the anointing of the Holy Spirit. I have often wondered about that teaching. Why would Jesus give up so easily? I mean come on; He is God, and He spoke with all authority. Was He ever tempted to knock some sense into these people by dropping a big "I am God!" hammer on their heads? Why did He simply witness and move on? I guess through omnipotence, He saw the big picture—a picture I am just now coming to grips with. He has the answers to the test, and He already knows the end of the story. I guess He realized spiritual awakening is a process for most. It takes time to cultivate in the recesses of our hearts. It grows rapidly and uncontrollably for some; though, for most, it is a series of unmistakable plantings. A good deed here, a witness by him, a sacrificial act by her, love personified . . . on and on, over time, the Holy Spirit plants and waters, plants and waters, until BANG, we get IT!

We have all seen the one who is a zealot for Christ. Usually, they are new believers; though sometimes, even we "veterans" possess the quality. They are out to save the world, through whatever means possible—they have found it, and come hell or high water, they are going to tell you about it. I can remember as a kid of about seven or eight, when my sister, Pattie, was radically saved, through the ministry of Chuck Smith and Calvary Chapel, and decided she was going to take on my father. Now, this was an interesting contest which lasted for what seemed like years to a kid; though, it probably lasted only a few weeks.

Pattie accepted Christ while attending a Calvary Chapel service. My father was a lifelong Roman Catholic. As Pattie became more confident in her faith, she became more vocal about her perception that my father did not know Jesus as his Lord and Savior, so he was doomed to hell. Now, considering the dynamics of my family discussed earlier, this meant fireworks whenever they were around each other, and man did it get hot at times. Pattie would go off on the Catholics "worshiping" the Virgin Mary or the veneration of saints, and my father would go off on the speaking in tongues and the "born again hippies disgracing the holiness of Jesus Christ and His church." All the while, they were disgracing both themselves and God.

They slowly realized changing each other's minds was not going to happen, so they eventually gave up the fight. Both my sister and my father recently passed away within a year of each other. I find it a little funny to think they are both in Heaven, side by side, with Jesus. I wonder if they ever thought of having to do that while they were in the heat of battle.

When is it that God can trust us? I believe it is simple. It's when we reach a point where we act according to God's Word and not our own—when we stop majoring in minors and start majoring in love. It is only when we come to the realization there is one true opinion that counts, that the only opinion that matters is God's—the opinion spoken to us in love through the Bible and the Holy Spirit dwelling in us. I think this is when one of those "I am God!" hammers should fall. Only when we get "it" does God truly begin to use us in big ways. The TRUTH of God's opinion is love, and it's a powerful thing.

So, what does it mean to major in minors? Let's explore it with a study of American Christian culture. We all know about the reputation of the "dreaded" Bible belt, the land of Christian do's and don'ts, Mecca for the Christian Fraternity—you are either in the club or you're out, and if you're in, you have to play by the rules, NO EXCEPTIONS. There will be no drinking, no smoking, no dancing, and no swearing. If you do, you're out! You are damned, you are scorned, and you probably never were a Christian anyway!

Now, in the defense of the Bible belt, I spent four years living in Oklahoma while attending Oklahoma Wesleyan University, an awesome Christian school, representing the truth of Christianity without excuse or compromise. During that time, I grew to know some of the most down-to-earth and lovely people I have ever met. To this day, over thirty years later, many of my best friends are "Bible Belters"; they are people who truly live the love of Jesus and serve Christ well.

Still, in "The Bible Belt," I also found a hotbed of Christian legalists, people who seemed to think that loving their neighbor was secondary to appearance, that reaching out and meeting a non-believer or even someone of a different Christian denomination was potentially dirtying to their Christian "witness." And certainly, being seen with someone who didn't follow the rules was as much of a "sin" as committing the "sin" yourself. It breaks my heart to think of how many people have not accepted Jesus because they thought they couldn't play by the rules or didn't have the correct attire for Sunday mornings. It also breaks my heart to think of how many Christian legalists missed opportunities to fulfill their callings so they wouldn't stain their reputations. I believe this overt disdain for God's people is as uncivil and repulsive as it is to yell, "Go to Hell! You aren't like me, so go to Hell."

The cultural reality of appearance over love was really brought to light for me when my mother would share about her childhood, growing up in Oklahoma during the Depression. Her family was very poor, affording her only one very tattered dress, not fit for Sunday church services. Also working against her was the fact that my grandfather left her family when my mother was very young, leaving my grandmother a divorcee and the entire family "unclean" in the eyes of many churchgoers of the day. It broke my heart that my mother never really felt comfortable in church, even in her last years when she had really embraced her relationship with Jesus. Because of her experience growing up, a church family was never a part of her spiritual journey. Had my mother felt adequate enough to embrace church, her life would have been richer, and God's calling on her life could have been fulfilled.

## Have I Mentioned God's Love?

*The Lord appeared to us in the past, saying: "I have loved you with an everlasting love; I have drawn you with unfailing kindness."*
Jeremiah 31:3, NIV

In the Greek language, one finds "Telugu Love," or "Finished Love." God's love is perfect. God's love is never failing. God pursues us with unconditional, no rules, no amendments love. It is an everlasting, complete love. It is simple: you accept it, and you receive it.

This kind of love can only come from God, whose presence and dominion is everlasting. He does not change. What this translates to is that you can always count on the love of God at all times, and in all situations, even when everybody around you has rejected you. I am reminded by the not-so-distant memory of a once very rich and very powerful Wall Street tycoon, Bernie Madoff. Bernie pulled off the largest Ponzi scheme in history and stole hundreds of millions of dollars from some of the smartest and most famous people of our time. Bernie collected investors by the hundreds in his very lucrative fund and promised uncommonly high returns. In the end, it was actually too good to be true, and it all crumbled around him. When Bernie's little game ended, so did all of his relationships. Bernie was and is still known as the pariah of the rich and wealthy. In the end, though, even Bernie Madoff has the assurance of the love of God. Bernie, if willing to accept, is as worthy of God's love as any of us.

God's love transcends time and space and extends to our descendants. We see this in the lives of people like Abraham and David. God loved them and blessed them, He made a covenant with them, and He promised that the blessings of the covenant would continue on to their descendants (us) forever, as long as they lived in obedience to His commandments. Long after the beneficiaries of God's love have died, those who come after will be able to enjoy that good seed that was sown. That is a wonderful privilege made possible by the love of God.

It is the everlasting love that God has for man that compels Him to never give up on us. If a person lives for eighty years, and leads a sinful life for seventy-nine years, eleven months, and twenty-nine days, and then gives his life to Jesus on his deathbed, God still forgives because of this divine, unexplainable, supernatural love. For as long as we breathe, the love of God abounds. Even though He hates the sin we commit, He still loves us. This divine love is why all of us are potential children of God.

Sometimes people without faith think love just comes naturally. The truth is God only makes love available to humans so we can see His goodness. Because of that, we come fully under His Lordship. God's love was very well understood by the earth's early people and by old traditions followed today around the world. The complexity of life today serves as a grand distraction when seeing God's love for us.

God's everlasting love makes Heaven possible. God actually wants us to come and live with Him in His Kingdom; hence, He has prepared Heaven for as many as are willing to come. Through the Holy Spirit and Jesus, God says *come*, but only through the acceptance of Jesus as your Lord and Savior will you inherit this gift. The Biblical description of heaven allows us to understand God is willing to give His very best to His children.

Jesus said, "Do not let your heart be troubled; believe in God, believe also in Me. In My Father's house are many dwelling places; if it were not so, I would have told you; for I go to prepare a place for you. If I go and prepare a place for you, I will come again and receive you to myself, that where I am, there you may be also" (John 14:1-3, NASB 1995).

We are not just joint heirs with Christ. He has the very best in store for us as future residents of heaven. There was no iota of jealousy in the voice of Jesus when He was making that statement. He does not regret that we are coming to share in His glory. He is willing and ready to share it with as many that want it, all because of love.

**The everlasting love of God will also make us to be like Him.**

*See how great a love the Father has bestowed on us, that we would be called children of God; and such we are. For this reason the world does not know us, because it did not know Him. Beloved, now we are children of God, and it has not appeared as yet what we will be. We know that when He appears, we will be like Him, because we will see Him just as He is. And everyone who has this hope fixed on Him purifies himself, just as He is pure.*
1 John 3:1-3, NASB1995

First, we will see Him as He is. That is a wonderful privilege. Up until now, only Jacob has seen the face of God (Genesis 32:30). Moses asked God to let him, and after much pleading and being hidden in the cleft of a rock, God allowed him to see only His backside. That experience alone made the face of Moses shine brighter than the sun. The children of Israel could not look into his eyes. He had to cover his face whenever he wanted to speak with them. By His love, we too, will be able to see God as He is when we get to Heaven.

Secondly, we shall be like Him. It is true; We are created in His image and likeness, but we do not fully carry His nature. When man fell in the Garden of Eden, we lost that, and we have been struggling with a sinful nature ever since. But when we get to Heaven, we shall be fully transformed, and we will discard this corrupt, mortal body for our glorious heavenly body. This scriptural reality is striking to me, almost surreal. If we read and accept any other Biblical claim though, we must also believe this to be true. How awesome this will be! Hopefully, I'll get my thirty-two-inch waistline back.

### The Love of God is a Free Gift

The truth of the matter is, we can not do anything to earn the love of God, so He has not asked us to try. His love comes freely to everyone who believes and accepts Him as Lord and Savior. God's grace is a free gift, period. That contrasts with all other major religions like Islam, Buddhism, or Hinduism, where you have to meet conditions or standards to gain the love of their god. And even after making all of the those sacrifices, you are really not sure whether you have received it or not.

For these religions, it is obvious that only some people will be able to attain the standards and rules to get the love of their gods. As they are laid out, we see that the majority of their followers, or mankind, in general, will fall short of meeting the standard.

The price for love paid by Jesus makes it possible for everybody on earth to be able to freely receive His gift. Jesus said anyone who comes to the Father will not be cast away—they will be attended to, all because of His great love and sacrifice for us.

This love can also be compared to the love a nursing mother has for her newborn child. The child has not done anything to deserve the mother's affection, or anything at all to make her say, "Let me devote myself to you or shower you with my unconditional love." The baby, up until this point, may have caused the mother discomfort, pain, and sleepless nights, yet the mother will love and continue to love unconditionally.

In the same way, God loves us, He loved Jesus in His humanity. Through the baptism by John the Baptist, God spoke to Jesus. The Holy Spirit descended on Him in bodily form as a dove. "And a voice came from heaven: 'You are my Son, whom I love; with you I am well pleased'" (Luke 3:22, NIV).

It is important to note that Jesus, at this point, had not really done anything in His ministry. No miracles, no healings, and no performance of any type, yet God tells Jesus He is loved and is pleasing in His sight.

God loves our calling in the same way He loves us. He created us to love Him, and He created our callings to fulfill His love for us. When we live out our callings, we receive God's love as perfectly as possible. We have heard it a thousand times in the Christian world: People who act out their faith, through serving others, are more blessed and fulfilled than those they served.

We need to act on this love if we want to fully benefit from it. My biggest struggle is inaction. Frankly, it is laziness! I am someone who embraces relaxation. It's in my DNA. God calls me, and my reflex is to take a nap. Unfortunately, it's who I am. Acting on God's call must be a conscious and deliberate effort for me. To act, I need to be focused on His love and not my comfort.

## Our Calling is God's Love

God's love is not conditional, but it does test us. It is challenging! Even Jesus was challenged and tested. He was sent to a horrible, painful death, in the fulfillment of God's love for us. Scripture tells us Jesus actually sweats drops of blood, a physiological condition called Hematidrosis, which can happen when a person is under intense pressure and anxiety. The sin of the world past, present, and future, was as heavy a burden as has ever been carried. Only unconditional love can withstand that load.

### A Calling of Integrity

God Almighty is a God of integrity. Everything about Him shows He will not compromise. Looking through the Bible, we see illustrations where His integrity stands out, even in situations where one would think He ought to have acted otherwise.

God showed integrity in the covenant He made with Abraham.

*Then Moses implored the Lord his God, and said, "O Lord, why does Your anger burn against Your people whom You have brought out from the land of Egypt with great power and with a mighty hand? "Why should the Egyptians speak, saying, 'With evil intent He brought them out to kill them in the mountains and to destroy them from the face of the earth'? Turn from Your burning anger and change Your mind about doing harm to Your people. "Remember Abraham, Isaac, and Israel, Your servants to whom you swore by Yourself, and said to them, 'I will multiply your descendants as the stars of the heavens, and all this land of which I have spoken I will give to your descendants, and they shall inherit it forever.'" So the Lord changed His mind*

*about the harm which He said He would do to His people.*
Exodus 32:11-15, NASB 1995

The children of Israel were descendants of Abraham, but unfortunately, they did not take after him in obeying God and in doing His will. They sinned, ceaselessly, against God in the wilderness, and according to the Bible passage above, God was ready to destroy them and discard their race. But when Moses pleaded with God, He heard and changed His mind, all because of the covenant that he had with Abraham, their father.

It is unlike God to allow a mortal man to alter His plan like Moses did, and it is unheard of that God would change His mind. But because of integrity alone, God inconvenienced Himself to allow a mortal man to turn Him away from what He wanted to do, despite the fact that He was fully justified to carry out His action. I can remember, as a kid, my father getting frustrated with my mother because we would "wear her out when asking for things." We would simply keep asking for whatever we wanted until she finally gave in, and it usually didn't take long. As we got older, we would actually tease my mother for always giving in to us when we were kids, and she simply said, "I love you too much to tell you *no* and mean it." What a lesson! Even though Abraham was not alive to accuse Him of going back on His word, God was faithful to love and to His promises to Abraham. He is God and can do whatever pleases Him in the affairs of men, yet, He doesn't because of His promises and love for us.

TEN

# Prayer Works

*For this reason it is by faith, in order that it may be in accordance with grace, so that the promise will be guaranteed to all the descendants, not only to those who are of the Law, but also to those who are of the faith of Abraham, who is the father of us all, (as it is written, "A FATHER OF MANY NATIONS HAVE I MADE YOU") in the presence of Him whom he believed, even God, who gives life to the dead and calls into being that which does not exist.*

Romans 4:16-17, NASB 1995

It is integrity that made Him willing to accept gentile sinners into His kingdom and allow them to share the same inheritance as those who were born as Jews. He promised Abraham that through him, all of the nations of the earth would be blessed. This He fulfilled in making all persons who believed in Him become His sons and have an inheritance in His Kingdom.

There was nothing in the life of Gentile sinners that would have caused God to consider them as candidates for Heaven and for eternal glory, except for their being His creation. But because of His integrity, God closed His eyes against the abominable things they did and allowed the blood of Jesus to make atonement for their sins, so they could be justified before Him.

## The integrity of God was revealed when Jesus hung on the cross

*About the ninth hour Jesus cried out with a loud voice, saying, "ELI, ELI, LAMA SABACHTHANI?" that is, "MY GOD, MY GOD, WHY HAVE YOU FORSAKEN ME?" And some of those who were standing there, when they heard it, began saying, "This man is calling for Elijah." Immediately one of them ran, and taking a sponge, he filled it with sour wine and put it on a reed, and gave Him a drink. But the rest of them said, "Let us see whether Elijah will come to save Him." And Jesus cried out again with a loud voice, and yielded up His spirit.*
Matthew 27:46-51, NASB 1995

The Son of God, who took away the sins of the world, was in agony and great pain for sins He never committed, and as was destined, He took this punishment. God had to turn His eyes away from His Son. The desolation was so overwhelming, Jesus cried out, "My God my God, why have you forsaken me?" (Matthew 27:46, NIV). God did not answer Him—not even a word of comfort or consolation came from the Father. The Son was abandoned in his dying, not because God is wicked, but because His eyes are too pure to behold sin, even when the sin was according to His plan.

This is a great lesson for us to heed. God did not spare His Son pain and discomfort while doing His will, so will He spare us if we go our own way and refuse to do His will? No, He will not spare our pain and discomfort. But, how reassuring that if we decide to obey Him in our calling and stand all out for Him, He is ready to stand by us.

## The Case of the Three Hebrews in the Land of Babylon

*Shadrach, Meshach and Abed-nego replied to the king, "O*

*Nebuchadnezzar, we do not need to give you an answer concerning this matter." If it be so, our God whom we serve is able to deliver us from the furnace of blazing fire; and He will deliver us out of your hand, O king. " But even if He does not, let it be known to you, O king, that we are not going to serve your gods or worship the golden image that you have set up."*
Daniel 3:16-19, NASB 1995

The three Hebrew boys Shadrach, Meshach, and Abednego suddenly found themselves confronted with death because they would not bow down to the idol of the king. It was a precarious situation for them, but they decided to hold onto their faith in God. They never minced words when they told the king, to his face, they would not bow down to his god—they believed God Almighty would deliver them.

These three esteemed Hebrew boys were young men who had never really experienced a divine encounter with God; at least, not as David, who held claim to killing a lion and a bear, and confronting Goliath. And not like Gideon, who was able to get his golden fleece wet after a discussion with God. Yet, the boys were able to hold to the untested, little faith they had in Him. This was why they said, "But even if He does not, let it be known to you, O king, that we are not going to serve your gods or worship the golden image that you have set up" (Daniel 3:19, NASB 1995).

This must have been a great opportunity for God to show He is the real God and not the golden idol of Nebuchadnezzar. God's plan was simple: He proved that the multitudes in the realm of King Nebuchadnezzar who worshiped the golden idol did so in vain. Our God is a jealous God, and He always shows the truth.

God had no choice but to defend His name on that day. What would have happened if the three Hebrew boys had been roasted in the fiery furnace of the king? That would have been a big blow to the reputation of God, and it would have been very difficult for Daniel to be able to prove to the king, as he did, that God Almighty is the only God, and He alone deserves to be worshiped.

*All the inhabitants of the earth are accounted as nothing,*
*But He does according to His will in the host of heaven*
*And among the inhabitants of earth; And no one can ward off His hand Or say to Him, ' What have You done?'*
Daniel 4:35, NASB 1995

In God's eyes, integrity means being what you claim to be and maintaining your stand, despite unfavorable conditions. God has only one nature—that of God!

*For I, the Lord, do not change.*
Malachi 3:6, NASB 1995

He has been the same for ages, even before Heaven and earth were conceived, and up until this moment, He has not changed one bit. He will remain so throughout eternity. He is the perfect example of integrity we must learn and dream to live by. God honors His word.

*For You have magnified Your word*
*according to all Your name.*
Psalm 138:2, NASB 1995

Real human integrity starts when we agree we are sinners and only saved by grace; when we reason together with God about our true nature, not according to how we and the world see it, but how God, who cannot be deceived, sees it.

*For all have sinned and fall short of the glory of God.*
Romans 3:23, NASB 1995

You can claim to be led into sin by people close to you like Adam did, or you can claim that people influenced you to live in disobedience as King Saul did, but God sees all and always calls us on it. God requires of us that we show our integrity by accepting His verdict as the Judge and Lord over our lives.

*Behold, You desire truth in the innermost being and in the hidden part You will make me know wisdom.*
Psalm 51:6-7, NASB 1995

David was called a man after God's heart because, in spite of all his wrongdoing, He was a man of integrity. When David was confronted by the Prophet, he immediately admitted he had sinned against God, and he immediately sought forgiveness.

**The Goal of a Blessed Life**

Man desires image, status, and admiration from other men—God desires integrity.

*Man looks at the outward appearance, but the Lord looks at the heart.*
1 Samuel 16:7, NIV

God is more interested in our motives and less about our actions because they usually dictate behavior. What you see is not always what you get with man, but that is *always* what you get with God. Transparency is very difficult for me, as it is for most. My wife reminds me of my pride when I keep "private" things private. As Community Leaders for up to fifty Saddleback Church small groups, we are taught to teach our leaders to inspire and encourage complete openness and transparency. The only way to really reach a level of intimacy and live together as a small group is to achieve an open and honest life, a tall order but very fulfilling when achieved.

Performing acts of kindness or serving in a ministry for appearances is self-serving and rarely fulfilling. Interestingly, though, God can use self-serving actions for His purpose. Think of the televangelist who is in it for the money, fame, and all things prideful. Is his work in bringing followers to the Lord fruitless? Not necessarily. The salvation of a Christian who was won through the ministry of a crook is as real as anyone else. All things are made good through the glory of God.

Confused by Pastor Rick's comments once, I really needed to process when he said that the motivations of a minister had nothing to do with the fruit they bore. In other words, a bad person can be just as effective in leading someone to Christ as a holy person can, and a crooked minister who pockets the offering for personal use can be just as effective in reaching people as Mother Teresa.

As a pilot in the private jet world, and especially in the Gulfstream Jet world, I can tell you there are few secrets among the pilots. This community of aviators is small and relatively exclusive, and as a member, I am privy to stories about celebrities, captains of industry, and even televangelists who fly around in lavish corporate jets for personal junkets. We see it all in those jets, and when that door shuts, everybody tends to let their hair down, and their true self emerges. Please, let me be clear, I understand how valuable personal jet transportation can be, and I certainly see a place for it when it comes to access and impact to spread the Word, but it can be abused.

Where Rick's words tested me was when I had to compare the integrity, antics, and attitudes of those abusers I know with the fruit of their ministry. I don't dispute the fact that they are the abusers He is using for His earthly purpose, but I find it difficult to come to terms with whether or not they are really faithful to their calling.

Clearly, with television comes a vast audience. It is perhaps the biggest tool God has ever had in spreading His word. Still, I want to believe that character and integrity preach the word better and more effectively than just striving to appear before crowds and be famous. I want to believe this is the main reason why Jesus had to live among God's people: so we could see everything about his life and acknowledge whether He was truly the Son of God or not.

It was recorded that even those who opposed Jesus did not have any concrete evidence to speak against Him. That is how it should be. How the Heavens must weep when a pastor or priest falls astray, and how many souls are lost in the process? As a plug for Pastor Rick—in over twenty years of attending Saddleback Church and being involved in various parts of leadership and living in the same community, I have never heard of even a hint of misconduct or impropriety. It only takes one bad apple to spoil the whole bunch, and there have been many bad apples in my lifetime.

*God blesses those whose hearts are pure,*
*for they will see God.*
Matthew 5:8, NLT

Again, I struggle with how God works and how He uses His people. The trait of integrity translates into wholeness, authenticity, and unmixed motivation. As illustrated through the lives and actions of God's heavy lifters, purity of character and lives of integrity is a process. This is the case for us as we develop our personal relationship with Jesus, and even as we work out our own callings. As purity takes over, we are pardoned, becoming people of integrity just like David, Moses, and Abraham did in their spiritual journeys. All of them chose bad actions but possessed good hearts, which eventually translated into integrity and service to God.

I have now come to the realization God is not only after "good" people, but anybody, good or bad, who accepts Him and His conditions for life. God wants us to come to Him, just as we are. He already knows how bad or good we are and all we do or have done. We can not hide anything from Him, for He knew us even before we were born. David was a man after God's heart, despite the fact he committed adultery and murder. God still trusted him to reign as King.

The goal of those who were blessed in the Bible was to please God. As they worked towards carrying out their calling, God helped them to achieve that goal by overcoming the obstacles that came before them. We are not only called to do the work of God and spread His message all over the world, but we are to live on earth as He did. Jesus came to show us how we are to live for God. He is the perfect pattern of what God wants us to be. We should continually strive to grow in our spiritual lives. This process of sanctification is ongoing and is only finished as we enter Heaven. Earthly challenges are met daily, but the reward of Heaven is final and complete.

The degree to which our personal ambitions and goals agree with God's laid-down principles will determine the extent to which God is with us in fulfilling our calling. The more we conform to His will in all areas of our lives, the easier it is for Him to put His stamp of approval on what we do, and the more His blessings follow. Goodness and mercy will only follow those who dwell in His presence, and those who do things that invite His presence.

## Our Integrity is Blessed by God

Being a person of integrity does not mean we are sinless or perfect. It means we act with the proper motivation and purpose. It means we put aside our own ways, selfish or otherwise, and do everything within our power to please God. Our motivation should be to represent God. For me, a sign of spiritual growth is how my desires fall closer to God's path than in the past. I am growing every day with this and am continually amazed at how my will is ever closer to God's way. When we act in God's name with integrity, we are blessed in the process. Acting with integrity allows us confidence in our actions and in our faithfulness; spiritual maturity is evident when we allow God to take over.

*Whoever walks in integrity walks securely,*
*but whoever takes crooked paths will be found out.*
Proverbs 10:9, NIV

Living a life of integrity not only saves us embarrassment, but it gives us assurance God will keep us safe from every unseen or spiritual foe. No matter where you live or who you live with, live a life of integrity. People want those of higher moral standards surrounding them, even if their life doesn't reflect those same moral standards. The first trait I look for when promoting or hiring someone is integrity. The truth is, it is much easier to find capable people than it is to find people who live a life focused on integrity.

**Spiritual confidence translates into personal stability**

*The integrity of the upright guides them, but the*
*unfaithful are destroyed by their duplicity.*
Proverbs 11:3, NIV

A heart of integrity gives us confidence in issues of life and puts us in harmony with God, as we strive to do His will. There is peace, joy, and confidence for everyone who obeys God— such confidence does not depend upon any physical or material possession and can not be affected by the absence of them.

There is a very natural order with everything God created, and living outside of the order creates conflict for anyone who is living in disobedience to His laws and integrity. Anyone living contrary lifestyles is destined to fall into their own trap, completely alienated from the plans and blessings of God.

### Integrity leaves a lasting legacy

*A righteous person lives on the basis of his integrity,*
*blessed are his children after he is gone.*
Proverbs 20:7, JUB

A life of integrity ensures your good name is preserved long after you are gone. Children learn from their parents. They inherit not only physical properties but also character and habits. We see this in the life of Timothy, who learns commitment to the things of God from his mother, who learned from her own mother. My father used to say, "The worst in us is like a generational curse handed to our children. Unless we consciously and prayerfully break the cycle, our sin will live on through our children. Battered children grow to be abusive parents, and abused children grow to abuse their children." In the same regard, Proverbs tells us we pass on curses from generation to generation. Teaching our children a life void of integrity is simply passing on a curse to them.

I was driving through town one day with a good friend. We had our children with us—his two boys and my two girls. With the kids in the back two rows of my mammoth

GMC Suburban, my friend and I discussed current events. He retorted with a diatribe of less-than-desirable words, especially for eight and ten-year-olds to hear. When I reacted to his language, used while in the kids' presence, his response was simply, "They don't hear what I am saying. They are too focused on each other." Well, you can imagine the look on my friend's face, and the look I gave back to him, when one of his kids burst out with the same profanity he'd used just a few minutes earlier. Let's just say, "I told you so" was included in my response. The incident, at the time, was kind of funny, and quite frankly, I received great satisfaction in being made right so eloquently and so promptly. But as I reflect, I grieve over the curse my friend was leaving for his boys. Fortunately, I can report my friend sorted out bits of his life and cleaned up his act in time to raise two wonderful young men. It's never too late.

When parents take time to train their children to live a life of integrity, they are giving them something more valuable than any monetary inheritance. The inheritance of Godly integrity will ensure they live a fulfilled life and impact the people around them, perhaps, most importantly, their children. God testified Abraham would guide his children and teach them concerning the ways of the Lord, so they would follow in his footsteps (Gen 18:19).

As always, God's plan is perfect, as Abraham was able to raise Isaac, a man of faith, who not only followed in his footsteps but also raised Jacob, who started the nation of Israel. Integrity will produce integrity, and no man can destroy a good seed that has been sown by God. Our investment in *stuff* withers. Our investment in the Kingdom of God (our calling) lasts for eternity.

*But if you pray to God and seek the favor of the Almighty, and if you are pure and live with integrity, he will surely*

*rise up and restore your happy home. And though you started with little, you will end with much.*
Job 8:5-7, NLT

**Integrity on earth translates into rewards throughout eternity**

*The master answered, 'You did well. You are a good and loyal servant. Because you were loyal with small things, I will let you care for much greater things. Come and share my joy with me.'*
Matthew 25:21, NCV

There is joy and a great reward for people of integrity. We see examples of people like Job, David, Joseph, Daniel, and others who reap the reward of integrity. Their names stand out through the pages of history for their blessed acts of integrity.

*O Lord, who may stay in your tent? Who may live on your holy mountain? The one who walks with integrity, does what is righteous, and speaks the truth within his heart. The one who does not slander with his tongue, do evil to a friend, or bring disgrace on his neighbor. The one who despises those rejected by God but honors those who fear the Lord. The one who makes a promise and does not break it, even though he is hurt by it. The one who does not collect interest on a loan or take a bribe against an innocent person. Whoever does these things will never be shaken.*
Psalm 15:1-5, GW

You may have a string of educational degrees, or be a highly decorated soldier, or you might have distinguished yourself in your field of study or career to the point of becoming an international celebrity. But, if you are living short of the standard set by God, all you have acquired will end with this world. Our divorce courts are full of people who lived for the moment, and our prisons are full of people who thought they were too smart to get caught.

Only through a life of integrity can we truly serve out our calling with blessing and lasting impact, but it is worth a pause to say that our past is in no way predictive of our ability to change and be blessed from today forward. God sees us each day, through Jesus, as a new creation.

As we know, there is nothing we sow on earth that will not go unnoticed. Every small act of kindness, a small prayer, or a smile to a stranger passing by is rewarded in Heaven. Likewise, everything you have been created and equipped to do which you fail to do will receive the judgment that is deserved (Rev 20:12). My friend and small group ministry partner, Eddie, likes to remind me that when we keep each other accountable, we often forget sins of omission. Knowing the right thing to do, but doing nothing or saying nothing, is as big a sin as actually acting in a sinful way. A life of integrity is as much about what we *don't do* as it is about what we do, and especially what we do when no one is looking.

Saint Augustine's message recognizes the first step toward personal integrity is the confession of our lack of integrity.[9] If we are to be real to our calling, first, we must work out being real to ourselves and real to others. Accountability can be especially difficult for men. We tend to think we can fix anything and must fix everything in our own power. I have been blessed with five men in my life who serve as my accountability partners. We can tell each other anything and expect each other to fess up to everything. Commitment to a group of people who keep us accountable is very important as we work out the fulfillment of our calling. I believe the Lord puts people in our lives to help facilitate Augustine's call to integrity. My biggest thanks to Charlie, Pete, Eddie, Bjarnie, and Brent for being those He placed in my life.

The truth is, whenever we are trying to deceive God, we are actually deceiving ourselves, because we are all naked before Him, and He knows us better than we know ourselves. He is so great, that we can not fathom His depth of knowledge and power.

## ELEVEN

# Imagination - The Workshop for Our Calling

Some of us know we are called by God. We have received a clear direction from Him concerning that which He has called us to, the assignments He has committed to our hands, and a general direction according to our gifts, and, as such, we can not deny the fact He wants to use us.

Most of the time, when we imagine our calling, we do not take the time to search deep into the seeds that are planted in us to get detail and a clear vision of what we really need. Some of us, including myself, just go ahead and leap into what seems to be the clear path. The writing of this book, for example, has been a bit of a marathon in sorting out, organizing, and finally completing. Had I really explored God's will and prayerfully sought the guidance and direction from the beginning that I have found in the end, it would have been so much easier to complete.

Finishing this book is a bit of a minor miracle in and of itself. Remember the part where God sometimes uses the most unqualified people to accomplish His will? I would love to hear the reactions of my high school English teacher or my Comp 101 professor at Oklahoma Wesleyan.

My lack of writing experience led to a lack of confidence, which led to the worst scenario for our callings—procrastination. Procrastination is perhaps the biggest thief of success, as we make the transition from imagination to action. Faith, or the lack of it, is a great petri dish for procrastination. This, in reality, is a travesty, as we rob ourselves, through inaction, of our partnership in ministry with God and all of the blessing that comes with it.

### The Trap of Procrastination and its Effects on our Calling

Some of us are outright lazy. We are not willing to go the extra mile for anything, including God. We live in a fast-food world, and we aren't willing to wait or work hard for much of anything. We treat our lives like the drive-thru window, and we expect everything quick, cheap, and loaded with sugar. Our laziness is an obstacle to the perseverance of a healthy prayer life, and it hinders a clear picture of what God wants for us. Procrastination has robbed many of us of the gifts and great anointing we could receive, all because we don't obey God's instructions. Our calling is God-sized, not our size. When we rely, completely and prayerfully, on His ability and not our own, we accomplish unimaginable things.

In Matthew 25, a master entrusted one talent of gold to a servant to invest. This was about twenty years of wage for the average worker (TLB). The master had given other servants much more to invest. They invested wisely and grew the wealth of the master, but the servant entrusted with the least to lose produced nothing in comparison. What does this parable mean? Some of us have buried what we have received from God, so we never produce. We do not multiply God's church because we falter, procrastinate, and get lazy in our calling.

### Inadequacy in our Calling

Moses argued with God; He felt he was not the right candidate for the assignment God had chosen for him. He told

God he was not an eloquent speaker, a skill necessary to help him convince Pharaoh that God actually sent him.

Try as Moses did, the excuse did not hold water with God. He saw the situation before choosing Moses. God is not looking for someone who is already perfect for a job. He only needs someone who is available and willing to say *yes*. God has the ability to make any person of His choosing become what He wants.

This is a lesson we must learn. When we are dealing with God, we must have the understanding He is the Almighty, the God of all creation, and impossibility doesn't hold meaning before Him. God knows all of our inadequacies before calling us, and no amount of argument or excuse that we muster can justify our refusal to heed His call. Rather, we are to seek His face and pray He will make us adequate.

I am reluctant to bring into discussion my wife's dirty little secret, but here goes: Valerie is riddled with a fear of public speaking in front of even small crowds. This has been a very big problem for her because she has answered the call to be a Core Group Leader for Community Bible Study. My wife must face her biggest demon weekly, as she answers God's call on her life. Over the years, it has become a bit easier for her, but, by no means, has she overcome the burden. I think she would say her dealing with the fear is God's way of keeping her aware that it is by His power and not her own that she is able.

## Our Calling and our Day Job

Work. What a great obstacle to seeing our calling through. Whether we are white-collar or blue, we can always come up with reasons to delay our calling. God will make a path whether we are busy or bored.

It always amazes me how God creates a clear path

when it comes to our calling. My wife, Valerie, is a CPA, but from 1993 until around 2012, she worked very little. A few summers ago, we decided it was time for her to go back to work. I had just started ClipperJet, and we were a bit stretched financially. Both of our daughters were in Private Christian college, so expenses were high, but life was more or less on autopilot, so it made complete sense. Valerie asked, "How will I find a job when I need to maintain my Community Bible Study responsibility on Tuesdays and Thursdays?" Oh, ye of so little faith! Remember the part where God is God? Almost immediately, through a little networking, she found out about a Christian business owner who needed a CFO for his small company. After a single interview, the job was hers, and Wayne, her new boss, has supported all her time off needs from day one.

I'll say it again, remember God is God. Many times in my ministry, I have let my schedule get in the way of meeting the obligations of my calling. After all, my job takes me all over the world. Many times in my career, I have lived with chronic jet lag and demanding bosses, needing to take kids to track practice, gymnastics practice, and volleyball practice, all in the same week. What I have found is simple—when I honor God by saying *yes*, He clears the path—my schedule clears, and the kids are taken care of. A note on the kid's part: I don't believe God ever expects us to sacrifice our parental duties as a cost of our calling duties. In fact, raising our children in the ways of God is our first calling. Focus on God's way, and let Him make the path straight.

I have found, in my life, that work has been an excuse in my ministry but rarely an obstacle. What I mean is, yes, travel gets in the way, but when I'm home, ministry requirements are usually set in the evenings and on the weekends, so work hours are rarely the reason we can't make it work. So why? It's simple. Being too busy or blaming work pressures is easy and an acceptable scapegoat. I can't say it enough: if you want your life to suddenly free itself of complexity, stress, and work pressure, then take the leap of faith, and act on what God is calling you to.

I can't say It strongly enough; don't let work get in the way of your calling. Work, with its many issues, is the reason many of us will not answer the call of God. There will never be a shortage of reasons. There is a need for us to get a better understanding of God's calling, or, should I say, God Himself. If we know God the way we ought to, we will not struggle with Him or our calling. Instead, we will count it a privilege to be called out of the multitudes that are in the world to partner with our Maker in His work, and we will gladly accept whatever role He wants us to play and do it with all that we have.

From the Old Testament to the New Testament, people have always seen God's calling to be too big, too scary, or too inconvenient. Clearly, we are the losers, when we turn God down. We will be the lesser for it. In or out, God's will is done. What you think you cannot do, someone else will do for Him, and maybe even better. No one is indispensable but God himself. I truly believe God gives us callings simply to build our faith or to bless us, and through our free will, we sometimes refuse to heed the call.

To be called by God is a privilege you must not despise or abuse. Most of the time, when people fail in their ministry, it is a result of the inability to deal with the flesh. The flesh will always get in your way, whenever you want to please God. Apostle Paul said, "I know that nothing good dwells in me, that is, in my flesh" (Romans 7:18, ESV). It is only after we put the flesh in its proper place that we can be free to do the will of God.

Our calling may be small and at the local church, or it may be a global reach assignment like our PEACE ministries at Saddleback, sending people all over the globe. They are all the same before God, and just like the parable of the talent,

He will give you according to your ability. He expects you to perform, as you rely on Him.

The question is, what do we need to get equipped for God's use? What will make us knock off procrastination and all those excuses that we tend to give in order to dodge God's assigned roles? The truth is, we can always find excuses to procrastinate—too little time, too few resources, or simply too little motivation. There are plenty of excuses, but more times than not, we fail to act on our calling because we have too little *faith.*

TWELVE

# Dare to Imagine

The word imagination emanated from the word *image*. It is having a picture of something that you desire in your heart. It is a very important topic in the Bible because it helps us to build faith in God, which is an essential ingredient in our Christian journey.

God used imagination when He was creating us. In God's magnificence, He simply spoke things into existence. The Bible recorded that God simply called those things that were not, as if they were.

*"By the word of the Lord the heavens were made, and by the breath of his mouth all their host."*
Psalm 33:4 ESV

Where did He call all things from? From His imagination, God breathed life where there was none. God already had a picture of the earth He wanted and the inhabitants that He would populate it with, and because He has the ability, He simply called on his imagination and built a world as would an artist creating a work of art. God's imagination fueled His creation.

God wants us all to learn from this as well. We all need to know how to use our imagination in order to fully grasp what He has in store for us. I believe that when we understand we were created in the image of God, His imagination is one of those characteristics.

This ability is a part of God He has decided to share with us. Remember we were created in His image, so imagination is clearly one of those God-to-man-only items. No other creature on earth is known to have an imagination. Animals or other creatures, apart from man, were not given this privilege, and it was not an oversight, but a specific design by God to make us equipped for the role we are to play as the landlords of His earth.

It is one thing for you to imagine things on your own. It is another thing for God to put a thought in your mind. You have God-inspired dreams, ideas, and aspirations. When you have this privilege, you will be able to think and imagine things that are beyond your human ability. You will catch a picture of things that ordinary human minds are not able to comprehend, and at that stage, if we can tap into the vision God has for us, we will move towards achieving impossible things for God. God does not imagine small things.

Scientists have discovered that our galaxy alone has over 300 billion stars in it, that is, if they try to limit it to what they have observed.

God is big. His imagination is incomprehensible, and when He decides to inspire us, He will ask us to do big things. Do not think of your own ability at all because it will be grossly inadequate for the task. He will supply all we need for the job.

He will not only inspire us; He will equip us to the fullest so we will not lack what we need for the work He wants us to do. If we could fully understand God's way, we would discover that for Him to call us is really His desire to draw closer to us. As He uses us, we will do extraordinary things for Him.

# Dare to Imagine

## Our Imagination Shapes our Life

We cannot rise above the level of our thoughts without God. If our mind's eye cannot see it, we have no vision. The reason God tells us to meditate in His words is to get us connected to His tremendous power that will deliver His blessings to us.

*. . . For as a man thinks in his heart, so he is.*
Proverbs 23:7, KJV

As you are thinking now in your heart, so you are. If you are thinking of failure, hopelessness, and impossibility, that is what you are, and that is what you will get. If you are thinking of success, peace, and prosperity, that is what you are, and that is what you will get. God is our sole source of power. I do not see this as the "Power of Positive Thinking" stuff preached in many churches and in many self-help books. It is the "Power of God-Thinking," and it should be the fuel that drives all Christians.

Referring back to my opening statements in the introduction, if we are ready for our callings, then the time has come for us to have a complete understanding of the importance of our thoughts. Many people do not care what goes on in their minds. Many believe it is natural for all kinds of thoughts to come and go and that it is practically impossible to tune your mind. Mind management is very difficult and a discipline that is rarely exercised because we are never challenged by what others can't see or hear. Our thoughts are ours and ours alone, so we think what we want. But remember, God is with us always.

*Be careful how you think; your life is shaped by your thoughts.*
Proverbs 4:23, GNT

One of the reasons God had to confuse the language of the people who built the Tower of Babel was to prevent them from having a common thought of achieving a goal that was contrary to His will. This tells us how powerful the thought of our hearts can be.

*The LORD said, "If as one people speaking the same language they have begun to do this, then nothing they plan to do will be impossible for them."*
Genesis 11:6, NIV

If God Himself can say this about human imagination, think of how powerful it could be and what great things we could achieve if we decided to partner with God.

### Imagination is Essential to a Faith

To build up a living faith, we must have imagination. We must be able to see the picture of what we want through our mind's eye. Faith in the mental picture gives us evidence of "things not seen."

*Faith is the confidence that what we hope for will actually happen; it gives us assurance about things we cannot see.*
Hebrews 11:1, NLT

Faith is an essential ingredient in answering our calling because we can only connect to God by faith. How can we know that God calls us to answer Him? It is by faith. How can we understand the call and link it with the specific tasks that God actually wants us to do? It is by faith.

The whole experience of walking with God is completed step by step, breath by breath (you get the idea), and it is all experienced through our imagination. Before he actually took the position, Abraham saw himself as the father of many nations. This is because God called him to it, and God gave him the image through his mind's eye.

*So we fix our eyes not on what is seen, but on what is unseen, since what is seen is temporary, but what is unseen is eternal.*
2 Corinthians 4:18, NIV

The things God has ordained for us in life may be things that can not be seen with physical eyes. Everything that is visible is temporary. This is a tough concept for non-believers. An imagination which, when used without God's priority, can really go astray and chase after selfish or ill-gotten wealth, fame, position, power, etc. But for the children of the Kingdom of God, things that are much more valuable than this are what He has ordained, and we can only see them through the eyes of faith. Please don't get me wrong, imagining wealth or fame or any good thing is not in question—it is where our unchecked imagination can take us in the pursuit of ill-gotten rewards.

### Great Lives Emanated from Great Dreams

*Where there is no vision the people perish . . .*
Proverbs 29:18, NIV

Most great people we see, who are called by God, do not become great suddenly. Rather, they have dreamt their way into greatness. These dreams are not the dreams of sleep, but rather the dreams of inspiration, of a burning inside the soul. God has placed a vision in their hearts and a desire to meet it head-on. They consciously refuse to accept a "substandard" level of living and aspire for greater and better lives through dreams of the soul and constructive imaginations.

## Whose Job is it Anyway?

*I pray that the eyes of your heart may be enlightened in order that you may know the hope to which He has called you, the riches of his glorious inheritance in His holy people . . .*
Ephesians 1:18, NIV

This prayer written for the Ephesian Christians, by the Apostle Paul, is applicable and meant for every child of God. There is nothing as frustrating as not knowing the reasons why He has called us and what we are expected to do. I must admit, this emotion has been real for me several times in my life. Perhaps, the most overwhelming point was when my time as an Air Force pilot was cut short. I could not understand having such a strong calling and having to move on because of circumstances out of my control. As I see the fabric come together in the tapestry of my life, I can now see what God saw all along. Our desires can sometimes lead us down a path away from our "purpose."

Everything God wants us to understand must be revealed to us in His timing, but we must be able to catch the vision and have it settled in our hearts. Hence, Paul prayed that all-important prayer for the Ephesians.

We must all remember that the calling of God is not our making but *His*. He is capable of bringing it to fulfillment. When we key into God-inspired imagination, we are bound to be great, because it is a call to greatness and into the mind of the Almighty who never does small things.

### God's Plan for my Life is Far Greater Than What I Can Imagine

We can never fully comprehend what God has in store for us. The Bible says, "What no eye has seen, what no ear has heard, and what no human mind has conceived, the things God has prepared for those who love him" (1 Cor 2:9, NIV). No matter how big or wild your personal dream for your life may be, it still can not match what God himself dreams for us.

*Now to him who is able to do immeasurably more*
*than all we ask or imagine, according to*
*his power that is at work within us.*
Ephesians 3:20, NIV

All children of God must aspire to imagination in order to achieve God's purpose for our lives. When we are dreaming big, we are honoring God, and we are also showing faith—the kind that can easily make the plan of our life come to *LIFE, His LIFE*. We must never stop imagining. The day we stop, we begin to die. The more we imagine, the more our vision and perspective broaden, the more we see beyond the realm of the physical, and the more we catch the vision of Heaven.

**The Imagination Called Doubt**

Doubt is definitely an enemy we must avoid, because it will greatly limit and weaken us in our ability to build our faith.

*If any of you lacks wisdom, you should ask God, who gives*
*generously to all without finding fault, and it will be*
*given to you. But when you ask, you must believe and not*
*doubt, because the one who doubts is like a wave of the sea,*
*blown and tossed by the wind. That person should not*
*expect to receive anything from the Lord. Such a*
*person is double-minded and unstable in all they do.*
James 1:5-7, NIV

Children find it easy to dream big. Children can imagine themselves driving a fire truck or sipping tea with their favorite doll. We need to become more like children when it comes to imagining things. We, adults, are more mature and have more experience, yet we find it difficult to imagine big things. One would think, with experience and maturity, we would cultivate even greater dreams as we age. What happens to us, and when exactly does it happen?

We must learn how to doubt our doubts and believe our imaginations. If we know how to build imagination, we will do well in our work for God, and we won't find it difficult to understand His ways.

Many Christians, even pastors, live under the yoke of doubt, and it has become a normal part of life for them. They find it difficult to believe in anything they can not see. Faith is drained as doubt has crept into their lives, ministries, and relationships. We must pray for the removal of our doubts, so we can start seeing the things God has for us. It seems simplistic to write this, and I am sure you are saying, "If only it were just that easy," but I truly think it is. The Holy Spirit is real and powerful and available. When was the last time you prayed, "God, please remove my doubt"?

*"If you can?" said Jesus. "Everything is possible for one who believes." Immediately the boy's father exclaimed, "I do believe; help me overcome my unbelief!"*
Mark 9:22-24, NIV

Mark 9:24 says, "I do believe; help me overcome my unbelief!" The father knew his problem was doubt, but he also knew Jesus had the power to help him trust and believe. Jesus did not condemn or reject the man's plea—He helped him because he made the attempt to seek faith.

God will show up when we act on faith.

### Fuel for Our Imagination – The Spirit and the Word

In what ways can God help our imagination grow? Our growth comes through His Spirit and His Word.

*And I will ask the Father, and he will give you another advocate to help you and be with you forever— the Spirit of truth. The world cannot accept him, because it neither sees him nor knows him. But you know him, for he lives with you and will be in you.*
John 14:16-17, NIV

When the Spirit of God is dwelling in you, it helps you start thinking like God. It happened to David when he was anointed by the Prophet Samuel, at his father Jesse's house, in 1 Samuel 6:1-13. He received a new heart, and from that day, he began to do extraordinary things. He was able to kill a lion, a bear, and even the giant Goliath could not stand before him.

The disciples were terrified after Jesus died. They could not muster the strength and courage to continue what Jesus left behind for them to accomplish. They had to hide from the Jews all the time. This continued until the day of Pentecost, when the Holy Spirit came on them and they spoke new tongues and received the kind of boldness no enemy could challenge.

When you combine the power of the Holy Spirit with daily quiet time and Bible reading, you will be inspired and discover new things as you dwell upon the word of God. Much of the inspiration I have received in writing this book comes from studying my sermon notes and Bible passages from weeks past. I routinely use sermon notes as my inspiration for meditation.

## Whose Job is it Anyway?

*Morning by morning he wakens me and*
*opens my understanding to his will.*
Isaiah 50:40, NLT

The more of the Word we have in us, the easier we find it to move ahead with God's calling for our life. Through the power of meditation and the help of the Holy Spirit, we keep expanding our vision until we are able to get the full picture of what God has ordained for our lives. Reflecting on active spiritual empowerment, it is clear to me there are two fundamentals we need to understand. First: God's timing is *not* always our timing. God routinely acts much slower than we hope. Second: through the Holy Spirit, we will have a deeply embedded dream. Deep, deep in our souls, will be a burning drive, vision, or "dream" of our calling.

I am the first to admit that my personal dreams, inspired by the Holy Spirit, have taken far longer than I ever thought they would to unfold. But the reality—the source of my "dream" or calling—has never wavered. Pastor Rick routinely tells the story of the dream of Saddleback Church and how God worked through him and Kay, his wife, to see the calling through the forty years to its present. It is truly the hand of God working through Pastor Rick's leadership that has created a model for churches around the world.

It's important to state again, without the MegaChurch movement started by only a few ministries around the country, including Saddleback, tens if not hundreds of thousands of people would not have been introduced to the saving grace of Jesus Christ. Think of the eternal impact of the MegaChurch movement around the world now and into the future. It can't be understated—millions of souls past, present, and future have and will be affected because of spiritual obedience and patience.

THIRTEEN

# Odds and Ends

As I have tried to formulate this text, it has been my goal to inspire those of us willing to be used by God for His great will. In the formulation, it dawned on me that not everything inspired can be neatly packaged or flow from paragraph to paragraph, so instead, let them stand alone as individual inspirations.

### Our Character is Important to God

*For this very reason, make every effort to add to your faith goodness; and to goodness, knowledge; and to knowledge, self-control; and to self-control, perseverance; and to perseverance, godliness; and to godliness, mutual affection; and to mutual affection, love. For if you possess these qualities in increasing measure, they will keep you from being ineffective and unproductive in your knowledge of our Lord Jesus Christ. But whoever does not have them is nearsighted and blind, forgetting that they have been cleansed from their past sins.*
2 Peter 1:5-9, NIV

God is not only interested in calling us to His work; He is interested in our character. Our character is important to God because the long-term blessing He has ordained for us is preparing us for Heaven and our everlasting life with Him.

## Whose Job is it Anyway?

The truth is, most of us are not even close to being ready for our promise. We all know His eyes are so pure, He can not behold sin, hence, we must ensure we live holy and in obedience to His will, no matter what gift or anointing we carry. God told Abraham, "Walk before me faithfully, and be blameless" (Genesis 17:1, NIV). God does not tolerate any act of ungodliness, no matter how small, as all unrighteousness is sin before Him. Only through the grace of God and His ultimate sacrifice through Jesus Christ are we able to walk faithfully.

In this regard, just as we are working to ensure we get the details of our calling right, we should also strive to get the fruit of the Holy Spirit working in our lives. Our gifts will allow us to operate in the power of the anointing, but grace will ensure we make it to Heaven, which is the ultimate calling for all Christians.

It is foolish to live like Samson, in the book of Judges, relying on his own power. Plan to live like Joseph, who lived by his fruit.

### A God Given Dream will be Connected to the Church and His Plan for the World

All of God's plans on earth will come to pass according to His own timing, His will, and His purpose for the church and all people. Our callings, even when they are business or school or raising children, must include a contribution to the kingdom. The calling of any individual is to work together with the church to achieve this. We are to play our own part in God's time and live it for the next generation.

*If you try to hang on to your life, you will lose it.*
*But if you give up your life for my sake and*
*for the sake of the Good News, you will save it.*
Mark 8:35, NIV

This alone will tell us how great the Almighty is. By His power, He has ensured that the church outlived all of the great nations and empires that we've read about in history, and even though the kingdom of darkness has never stopped raging against the church, it has never succeeded in prevailing against her. As Jesus saw His time was near, He gave His disciples the Great Commission—that is, the power, authority, and command to preach the gospel. This is our primary duty, no matter the area of our calling. In all that we do, we must be a witness to the Lord's truth.

Soul winning is spiritual fruit bearing—the former leads to the latter, and it is those who bear fruit that God will actually make full beneficiaries of His glory, now and forever.

In the end, after all the hate and disdain, God wins.

### We are Called to be Charitable

Here is where I don't understand regarding the behavior of most of the world—we chase all kinds of things in the pursuit of happiness: fame, fortune, and material possessions of all kinds. But in the end, there is no more joyful place, no cooler feeling, and no bigger high than a selfless act of charity. We have heard it a thousand times. People, rich and poor, sick and healthy, say they are most fulfilled when they are serving others, yet, for most people, it never sinks in. They don't get it either because they simply don't want to or because they are so self-centered they refuse to. It's our responsibility to grow past writing a check and expecting others to do the work of God. We are called to DO THE WORK!

Charity is a beautiful expression of us being the arms and legs of God. Most just don't take the time to learn about its impact or don't hear about the impact of charity in everyday lives. Simply put, most people don't allow charity to transform them as they see it transform others.

### We Are Called to Live with Credibility

This could arguably be the single most difficult challenge set forth in this book. Credibility is more of an art than a science—we earn credibility over time, and it will be easier for some. Credibility is a slice of your life that is not only public, it's also private. It's what you do when nobody's looking. It's what you say when you think your kids can't hear or aren't listening. It's living with honor even though nobody sees it. Your toughest critic should be you. Credibility is one of those weird things in life that can never be fully explained, but you know it when you see it!

### We are Called to Renewal

The Church is over 2000 years old, older than any corporation or government. The church has roughly 2.6 billion people who claim to follow Jesus Christ, which is nearly 1/3 of the world's population.[10] It is larger than any single ethnicity and larger than any nation. It is larger than the combined population of China and India,[11] the two most populous nations in the world.

The Church, and especially new churches in a community, have the responsibility to be the mother of a movement and reflect "renewal." The protestant reformation is the renewal that lives today. The "Going Global" push is everywhere; Every corporation is going global, our economy is now global. It's time to move the American church from self-centered consumerism to unselfish contribution to the global glory of God.

*But the Lord says, "don't dwell on your success of the past, do not cling to events of the past or dwell on what happened long ago. Watch for the New Thing I am going to do. It is happening already – you can see it now"*
Isaiah 43:18-19, GNT

## Odds and Ends

Pastor Rick routinely says it like this: "Any church who says that they are big enough and that they do not want to grow is really saying to their neighbors, 'You can go to hell.'" Church leaders must embrace renewal.

A base will only allow sand to pile so high before it spills over. The only way to avoid losing people is to continually broaden the base.

### The church is responsible for three things: preach, teach, and serve

*And have put on the new self, which is being renewed in knowledge in the image of its Creator. Here there is no Gentile or Jew, circumcised or uncircumcised, barbarian, Scythian, slave or free, but Christ is all, and is in all.*
Colossians. 3:10-11, NRSV

You don't have to be perfect. You don't even have to be correct. I believe you do have to be innovative. Less gossip and more collaboration between churches. Less putting down other theologies, more building of the CHURCH. As a whole, Jesus called the church His Bride, not His Brides! We are God's church and should be unified as one.

*Now I exhort you, brethren, by the name of our Lord Jesus Christ, that you all agree and that there be no divisions among you, but that you be made complete in the same mind and in the same judgment.*
1 Cor. 1:10, NASB 1995

### Obstacle to Our Calling: "Pride"

I'm going to tread on the always sensitive subject of pride, a subject which I know a little bit about, or if you ask my wife Valerie, a lot about—especially in my younger years. I truly believe it is pride that keeps most Christians from stepping out and embracing lay service or leadership. I'm not talking about selling everything and moving to China, the Czech Republic, or Siberia. I'm talking about leading a small group, teaching Sunday school, or even setting up chairs or working in the nursery. You can't let yourself get in the way of your work for God, your ministry! People are so easily distracted by their laziness (sense of self), their ego (sense of others), or their discomfort (sense of confidence).

**Our Calling Comes with a Catch!**

It is impossible to discuss this level of living by faith and reaching a point in our Christian walk where we are ready to act on our calling without talking about the elephant in the room. We tell a half-truth when we witness to people and lead people to a walk with Jesus Christ as their Lord and Savior without revealing it will not be all victory with joy and peace beyond understanding all of the time. Sure, it is joyful and peaceful, but to really live out a Christ-centered calling, we all must spend a bit of time in the desert, waiting on God and questioning why we must endure the refiner's fire. I am there right now, as I write these words. We study big and scary theological words like "sanctification" and wonder what that really means. I can tell you from experience that you learn exactly what it means when you're living it.

As with David, we will all see a bit of despair in our walk. We will all seek the face of God and ask Him if He has abandoned us:

*Psalm 143 - A Psalm of David. LORD, hear*
*my prayer, listen to my cry for mercy;*
*in your faithfulness and righteousness*

*come to my relief. Do not bring your servant into judgment, for no one living is righteous before you. The enemy pursues me, he crushes me to the ground; he makes me dwell in the darkness like those long dead. So my spirit grows faint within me; my heart within me is dismayed. I remember the days of long ago; I meditate on all your works and consider what your hands have done. I spread out my hands to you; I thirst for you like a parched land.[a] Answer me quickly, LORD; my spirit fails. Do not hide your face from me or I will be like those who go down to the pit. Let the morning bring me word of your unfailing love, for I have put my trust in you. Show me the way I should go, for to you I entrust my life. Rescue me from my enemies, LORD, for I hide myself in you. Teach me to do your will, for you are my God; may your good Spirit lead me on level ground. For your name's sake, LORD, preserve my life; in your righteousness, bring me out of trouble. In your unfailing love, silence my enemies; destroy all my foes, for I am your servant.*

Psalm 143, NIV

As David cries out to God, it is clear his devotion is not without conflict, pain, and foreboding. Despite David's devotion to God, he endures much, as God prepares his heart. For me, waiting on God is a painful reality. God says, "In My time, not yours; in My way, not yours, and in My will, not yours." Many theologians have referred to the sanctification process as the "refiner's fire" that separates our bad from our good and kneads away that which is not necessary for our calling to be effective. The term "refiner's fire" comes from the process of melting earth. Through the application of superheat, the molecules are hyper-excited and then separate. They leave the heavier molecules such as gold at the bottom, and other minerals and impurities float to the top and are discarded by the smelter.

Growth, as a Christian will, without a doubt, include pain and a bit of suffering. We are not immune to the human condition, but we are also subjected to a new process which is designed to help us relate better to those we serve, help us grow in our faith, and most of all, help us reach a new level of intimacy with Jesus, as we surrender everything to God. I have found no better explanation of this process than that presented by Pastor Lon Solomon, Pastor of McLean Bible Church, and author of the book Brokenness. If you find yourself relating to Job, then read Brokenness. This book will put it all in perspective.

FOURTEEN

# A Calling is Like Art - Sometimes Lonely

The Kingdom of God is vast, and our callings take on many forms, including assuming some of the tasks required but never seen. I spent about five years showing up on Saturday evenings to set up chairs for Sunday morning services. This was a calling that had no notice, no fanfare, and to be honest, it was one I often dreaded. The only upside was sharing the pain with a friend, John, giving us the opportunity to grow closer. It's the little stuff in ministry that makes the big stuff work, and real life isn't much different.

In my line of work, one finds himself in Rome, Italy, more often than most. While stumbling around in a half-jet-lagged state of consciousness, it dawned on me, just a few hundred feet from the Colosseum, that much like art, our callings are often a lonely place. Much of ministry is not seen or heard. On Sunday mornings, people often just walk into service, not realizing the amount of work it takes for the church service to work. Back to Rome: When you walk the streets of the Old Town, works of art are everywhere. Ruins on one corner, while there is a masterpiece of a marble statue across the street, and it is all overlooked as people go about their day.

Entrenched in the mess of ancient ruins and architecture ten times older than America, I was gobsmacked with the reality of our calling being lost in the ruins. Here is what I mean—it's about midnight, and the streets of Rome are still saturated with people. Most are like me, trying to acclimate to the many time zones. Along with the tourists are the street vendors selling trinkets of almost every proportion, from statues of the Pope to keychains with the Italian flag. But, I am attracted to street painters using spray paint to create art. On this evening, there are three guys painting exactly the same thing—a modern art combination of the ancient ruin and outer space, somehow melding in the red, white, and green of the Italian flag. As I observe the crowd, everybody flocks to only one artist, leaving the other two alone in their work.

This was interesting to me. What was different about the artist, the work, the colors, and the picture? There was no distinguishable difference. Even the painters appeared to be virtually the same person, sharing roughly the same age, general looks, quiet personalities, ethnic appearance, build, and artistic skill. Yet, one artist had a crowd of about thirty or forty people, and the others had virtually no crowd at all.

I think service and ministry can be very much the same. Some perform their callings with much fanfare and attention, while most simply go unnoticed. But in the eyes of God, even the most mundane task in His name is a bright light and pleasing to Him; perhaps even more pleasing. Mother Theresa spent the vast majority of her ministry without any public understanding of who she was or what she did. God used her in a mighty way, and through that sacrifice, her ministry was blessed.

*. . . I don't cling to my life for my own sake. The only value I place on my life is that I may finish my race, that I may fulfill the ministry that Jesus our King has given me, that I may gladly tell the good news of God's grace.*
Acts 20:24, VOICE

## A Calling to Change

Some time ago, I was invited to speak to a group of ministerial students at Oklahoma Wesleyan University. I opened the lecture with a pretty controversial statement. It was simple: "The traditional missionary is rapidly becoming obsolete." You can imagine how this statement went over with a group of young, ambitious college students preparing for their life's journey in ministry–the fulfillment of God's calling on their lives, their passion. I immediately got their attention. You should have seen the reaction on the face of the professor, who also happened to be the Director of Missionary Studies at the University. He had his head down looking at some papers in a manila folder, and his head popped straight up like a jack in the box. He was sitting at attention in an instant.

Knowing I had only about 3.2 milliseconds to recover before the shock factor wore off and the challenges started flying, I quickly stated it was all about the Math. I explained that the numbers don't lie, they don't add up, and they never will if we continue with the status quo. Here's why: There are not enough institutions of theological and missionary studies to produce enough vocational pastors and missionaries to fulfill the great commission. There are billions of people in the world who need to hear the good news, and that number is growing by hundreds of thousands of new human births each day. There are too few schools producing too few vocational missionaries each year. The work of the missionary must transform from not just preachers and evangelists to teachers and lay leadership. I have complete respect for all Christian Missionaries and their callings. Most of them have given up relatively comfortable lives for third-world poverty and simplicity. God has been well-served by them.

Still, we must empower and release the work to local lay leadership who must step up and accept their ordination in the same way that hundreds of thousands before them have.

Not just in Africa, but everywhere, in "all the nations." The Pastors and Vocational Missionaries must delegate to the locals who are spiritually ready and focus on the spiritual growth of new Lay Leaders. In the technology consulting business, we call it, "Train the Trainer." We implement software, then teach a functional "super user" to teach the rest of the team how to use the system. We must empower lay ministers to take on the next phase of God's work as we reach for the fulfillment of the great commission.

The good news is in the numbers as well. There are 2.2 billion people in the world who claim Jesus Christ as their Lord and Savior, and that number is growing every day. That number is bigger than the populations of both India and China, the two most populous nations in the world. The "New" church must be the mother of a movement, a movement of lay ministers taking their responsibility in the Kingdom of God, forging new ground, and accepting their calling, a calling of personal ministry for every believer.

**Final Thought**

*If I speak in the tongues of men or of angels, but do not have love, I am only a resounding gong or a clanging cymbal. If I have the gift of prophecy and can fathom all mysteries and all knowledge, and if I have a faith that can move mountains, but do not have love, I am nothing. If I give all I possess to the poor and give over my body to hardship that I may boast, but do not have love, I gain nothing.*
1 Corinthians 13:1-3, NIV

**Our Calling is to SERVE WITH LOVE!**

# Notes

1. Warren, Rick. *The Purpose Driven Life: What on Earth Am I Here For?* Grand Rapids, Michigan: Zondervan, 2002.

2. Guinness, Os. *The Call: Finding and Fulfilling the Central Purpose of Your Life*. Nashville, Tennessee: Thomas Nelson, 2003.

3. Guinness, Os. *The Call: Finding and Fulfilling the Central Purpose of Your Life*. Nashville, Tennessee: Thomas Nelson, 2003.

4. Dawkins, Richard. *The God Delusion*. Boston, Massachusetts: Houghton Mifflin Harcourt, 2006.

5. Rehnquist Court. *MCCREARY COUNTY, KENTUCKY, ET AL. V. AMERICAN CIVIL LIBERTIES UNION OF KENTUCKY ET AL., 545 U.S. 844*. 27 June 2005, www.thefire.org/first-amendment-library/decision/mccreary-county-kentucky-et-al-v-american-civil-liberties-union-of-kentucky-et-al/.

6. Fazal, Naeem. *Ex-Muslim: How One Daring Prayer to Jesus Changed a Life Forever*. Nashville, TN: Thomas Nelson, 2014.

7. Watson, Benjamin. 2014. "I'M ANGRY because the stories of injustice that have been passed down for generations seem to be continuing before our very eyes." Facebook, November

26, 2014. https://www.facebook.com/BenjaminWatsonOfficial/posts/602172116576590.

8. Piper, Everette, interview with O'Reilly, Bill. The O'Reilly Factor, Fox News Channel, April, 2015.

9. Saint Augustine. "The Project Gutenberg eBook of The Confessions of Saint Augustine, by Saint Augustine." Project Gutenberg, May 5, 2023. https://www.gutenberg.org/files/3296/3296-h/3296-h.htm.

10. "Real Time World Statistics." Worldometer, www.worldometers.info/. Dawes, Zach. "Global Christian Population Projected to Reach 3.3 Billion by 2050," Good Faith Media, February 13, 2023, https://goodfaithmedia.org/global-christian-population-projected-to-reach-3-3-billion-by-2050/#:~:text=The%202%2C604%2C381%2C000%20estimate%20for%20mid,than%20the%202022%20report's%20estimates.

11. "Population Comparison: China, EU, USA, and Japan." Worldometer, www.worldometers.info/population/china-eu-usa-japan-comparison/.

# Acknowledgements

I should take a few lines to acknowledge everyone who inspired me. For as long as I can remember, my parents always ensured I was fed with the knowledge and understanding that Jesus was real and His love was for me. As I grew, I was blessed with a young coach in junior high and high school, Ron Whitehouse, who professed his faith in Jesus and introduced reliance on Him in a practical way. Looking back, Coach Whitehouse was the first "lay" person I knew who lived out his calling daily as a lay minister. Whether he knew it or not, he was called to do exactly what he did: influence young, impressionable people for Christ. Valerie Harrell, later to become Valerie Occhipinti, won my heart as a college freshman when I was searching for meaning and a purpose. Valerie had a faith and conviction I had never seen in a person before. I believe that is what attracted me most to her; as our relationship grew, she challenged me to explore my own beliefs and mature a faith that had been dormant for far too long. Valerie's dedication to her calling as a lay minister with Community Bible Study Leadership and her family as a work for the Lord has inspired me throughout our 39-year marriage. Most people can say they are proud of their kids or love them, but, for me, I am all of that and inspired by my kids. Both of my daughters and their husbands are headlong into actively living out their callings as lay ministers every day. Alecia is a 30-year-old mother of 2 with a great husband living for the Lord. Alecia and Justin embrace their callings as lay ministers in our small church, doing whatever is asked and actively seeking to serve wherever needed. As for my daughter Tori and her husband Gui, I am delighted to see them grow in every way. As they start their family with a little boy on the way, they are amazingly committed to spiritual growth, church leadership, and leading their small group, striving to meet their every need. I look at all four of them and am blessed by their work for the Lord.

At Saddleback Church, there is every opportunity to serve. Pastor Ron Wilber was just the coach I needed to help me understand the importance of small-group ministry; he guided me as I developed into a Community Pastor serving many small groups. And finally, I must remember my friend Pastor Steve Rutenbar; Pastor Steve served as the Pastor of Mission and Disaster Relief at Saddleback for over 20 years! He personally led over 5,000 people "Lay Ministers" on hundreds of mission and PEACE trips to over 40 countries. He dedicated his life to sharing the Gospel and love of Jesus Christ around the world and transformed the lives of countless people. Pastor Steve leaves a legacy of Lay Ministry, motivating thousands to embrace their callings.

# About the Author

James is not an ordained pastor, evangelist, missionary, or author. He is a businessman and aviator who was called to write about the importance of lay ministry. James is the husband to Valerie Occhipinti Harrell, a father to Alecia Davenport and Tori Hadlich, and the Grandfather of Henley and Zeland Davenport and, of course, Baby Hadlich yet to be born. James served as a community leader and lay pastor to 26 small group leaders in Saddleback Church's Small Group ministry. Over the last three decades in lay ministry, James has served in almost every capacity within a traditional ministry structure, from nursery worker rocking babies during Sunday service to short-term missionary in Africa, and from ordained elder to Sunday morning church set up and Sunday School teacher. As a family, James and Valerie have hosted and led a small group bible study in their home for over two decades and are dedicated to living a life of love for family, friends, coworkers, and neighbors. Professionally, James has over twenty-five years of aviation operations management experience and has worked around the world as a leading operational efficiency and technology expert. In addition to ClipperJet Aviation CEO responsibilities, James is the Co-Founder of Consolidated Air Support Systems Inc. (CASS), an Aerospace/Airline consulting firm specializing in air operations management and air mobility. CASS is contracted with the Defense Department, working directly with Air Force Strategic Planning at the Pentagon and many Defense contractors and Aerospace companies to provide cutting-edge and transformational solutions to complex aviation business problems. James' work in aviation includes both the flight crew and passenger experience. As the Vice President for Sales and Customer Support (Europe, Middle East, and Africa) for Interactive Flight Technologies Inc. and the Director for US Domestic and Asia Pacific at BE Aerospace, Mr. Occhipinti helped shape the market introduction of advanced technology personal In-flight Entertainment systems. James was client-focused as he established the IFT company presence in London and expanded the client support focus in the region. As a Principal for the world's largest airline operations and technology consulting firm, AMR Consulting, a division of American Airlines, James provided technology solutions in Air Operations and Passenger Services to over one hundred and fifty airlines and aviation organizations in over fifty countries. James has authored industry papers on Airline Safety in a Deregulated Environment, Current Trends in Airline Automation, Modern Airline System Operations Control Methodologies, and also co-authored AERO-NAFTA Industry Impact, as well as the Flight Operations Management curriculum used at the IATA (International Air Transport Association) Institute of Air Transportation. He has been recognized as a leading industry speaker for airline safety and operational efficiencies. Additionally, Mr. Occhipinti has developed a varied background in higher education technology, providing Enterprise Resource Planning and Financial Systems consulting and services to major universities and colleges across the United States. These Higher Education-based software offerings revolve around business efficiency studies and recommended methodology improvements for efficient enterprise and student service operations. James is an FAA licensed Airline Transport Pilot with Turbojet and line flying experience. James served as a commissioned officer in the United States Air Force. James graduated from Oklahoma Wesleyan University with a Bachelor of Science Degree in Business Administration, Minor Studies in Computer Science, and a graduate with distinction from the IATA Institute in Geneva, Switzerland (Flight Operations Management Course). James has served as CEO and Chairman of the Board of ClipperJet Inc. He serves on the Board of Directors for HRBoss, a Singapore-based ERP Software Company, on the Board of Trustees for Oklahoma Wesleyan University, on the Board of Directors for the Oklahoma Wesleyan University Foundation, and as Chairman of the Board and CEO for Humanitarian Airlift International, a 501c3 Non Profit.

Printed in the USA
CPSIA information can be obtained
at www.ICGtesting.com
CBHW051117240624
10560CB00021B/147